FRANCIS JENKINSON

Francis Jenkinson
Librarian of Cambridge University

FRANCIS JENKINSON,

Fellow of Trinity College Cambridge and University Librarian.

A MEMOIR

by

H. F. STEWART,

Fellow of Trinity College Cambridge.

Cambridge
AT THE UNIVERSITY PRESS
mdccccxxvi

HE has achieved success who has lived well, laughed often, and loved much; who has gained the respect of intelligent men and the love of little children; who has filled his niche and accomplished his task; who has left the world better than he found it; who has always looked for the best in others and given the best he had; whose life was an inspiration; whose memory is a benediction.

M · C · J

E · L · J

NEC NON ET AMICIS

QVORVM NVMERVS INNVMERVS

HOC MNEMOSYNVM

CAPITIS

QVO CARENDO DIDICIMVS

QVANTVM CARVM AMISERIMVS

D · D · D

AVCTOR

CAMBRIDGE
UNIVERSITY PRESS

University Printing House, Cambridge CB2 8BS, United Kingdom

Published in the United States of America by Cambridge University Press, New York

Cambridge University Press is part of the University of Cambridge.

It furthers the University's mission by disseminating knowledge in the pursuit of education, learning and research at the highest international levels of excellence.

www.cambridge.org
Information on this title: www.cambridge.org/9781107690028

© Cambridge University Press 1926

First published 1926
First paperback edition 2013

A catalogue record for this publication is available from the British Library

ISBN 978-1-107-69002-8 Paperback

PREFACE

Two years have passed since Jenkinson was taken from us. My only excuse for the delay in bringing out this small volume is less leisure and nervous energy than I could wish to command. Now that it is done I am very conscious of its insufficiency. But such as it is I offer it to his many friends, named and unnamed in its pages, by way of remembrance.

H. F. STEWART

Trinity College
Michaelmas Day, 1925

CONTENTS

PORTRAITS

FACSIMILES

FRANCIS JENKINSON

Chapter I

SCHOOL DAYS

IF the memory of Francis Jenkinson, dear beyond expression to his intimate friends, seems to deserve celebration outside their circle, it is not because of the incidents of his quiet student's life, nor for any part played by him in public affairs, nor for any single conspicuous literary or scientific achievement. It is because of the richness and the swift success of his intellectual adventure, and, most of all, for the extreme beauty of his character.

There are, according to Pascal, three orders of greatness—of the world, of the mind, and of the heart. In two of these Jenkinson was pre-eminent. Indeed, to many who knew him best, he seemed to come as near perfection, mental and moral, as is possible on earth.

He was not a creative genius; but his manifold and always first-class accomplishment, his unerring and immediate response to every aesthetic appeal, indicate an intelligence of uncommon power and a very high artistic endowment, while I believe him to have been incapable of a consciously wrong thought or unkind act. His practice was a proof of Plato's generalization—κακὸς ἑκὼν οὐδείς.

The stuff out of which these inner qualities were wrought was inherited from his parents no less than his tall figure, and his refined and delicate features. His father, John Henry, was the younger brother of Sir George Samuel Jenkinson, 11th Baronet, of Hawkesbury, and second son of Dr John Banks Jenkinson, Bishop of St David's, and Frances Pechell of Berkhampstead Hall. *Bien né et bien fait*, John Jenkinson was an ardent lover of nature and a water-colour painter who only lacked training to reach a high rank in his art. His wife, Alice

Gordon-Cumming of Altyre, was, as befitted the great-grand-daughter of the incomparable Betty Gunning, one of the most beautiful and charming women of her day. From both sides then, from Jenkinsons and Pechells, Campbells and Cummings, came a general culture and a devotion to natural history, art, music, and literature, which was developed to a very unusual degree in the subject of this memoir.

Under the emotion caused by his wife's accidental and tragic death in December, 1859, when Francis was six years old, John Jenkinson took orders and went as voluntary curate to Mr Arthur Pusey-Cust (afterwards Dean of York) at St Mary's, Reading. He lived with his children and their faithful governess, Miss Ann Hustler, in the vicarage which the Custs surrendered, thinking it too near the churchyard for health. But the Jenkinsons were well and happy there, and there they remained all through the boy's schooling. In 1872 John Jenkinson, being dislodged from the vicarage by a new vicar, left Reading and went wandering for eleven years, till at length he settled at Crowborough in 1887 where he died in 1914, aged 91. He was not an ordinary parson, but he was a man of active charity and compassion, who literally washed the feet of the poor, and scandalized convention by cutting the toe nails of the bedridden old women of his parish.

Francis went to school at Mr Nind's, Woodcote, near Henley-on-Thames, from 1863 to 1865, and at Marlborough from October, 1865 to 1872. Woodcote was within easy reach of his father, and he could get him over for the day to look at some bird's nest in a forbidden area.

I wish you would come over to see me, for today I saw two birds like some kind of hawk fly out of a tree which is just out of bounds, and if you come over we can go out together, and get the eggs; in the same tree are a chaffinch's nest and a bigger nest which I think is a Missel Thrush. PLEASE COME. I have a Blackbird's and an egg which I think is a Blackbird but I am not sure; besides I am in a great hurry to shew you my other egg. I send you a piece of the nest which I told you about.

FRANCIS JENKINSON   *with his father*

January 1860

He wore a kilt and was teased accordingly, but he was not unhappy. The boredom of which he sometimes complains by letter—"We go out for walks, but I would just as soon be in the playground; we are driven along like a flock of sheep"—was redeemed by work which he finds interesting—"I like Xenophon very much"—and especially by the joys of bird's-nesting, all the sweeter for being illegal. "You said you were very glad that we were allowed to look for nests. We aren't, for we should get it, if we were found out."

There are echoes of fisticuffs. Stuart Donaldson, late Master of Magdalene, his very good friend, used to tell of an encounter in which Jenkinson was the aggressor—he was somewhat pert—and was properly punished. His letters are to a large extent common schoolboy form—demands for cake and apples, anticipations of holidays, news of play and work, visits of the hairdresser, etc., but they also declare the budding naturalist and collector, and are full of appropriate records, questions, and aspirations.

I have seen a brimstone, a tortoiseshell, a red admiral, a peacock, a small and a large garden white.... There is a boy here who has got 600 ancient coins, 200 of which are silver. I wish I had. Will you ask if my lupins are up and tell me? How is my hemp and corn getting on?

He does not shrink from the Latin names of shells picked up at Scilly (the first of his many visits there which he recalled was in 1857): *Bulla obtusa, Patella graeca, Bulla cylindrica, Tellura crassa, Fissurella reticulata.*

His musical taste begins to shew—"Yesterday we had that hymn called Martyrdom"—and his frankness of criticism, as *e.g.* when, the subscription for a schoolmaster's present not forthcoming from home, he describes his father's letter as "most unsatisfactory"; and, finally, the tender consideration for others which was his mark through life.

I wish you would go to Ravenscroft [a general dealer at Reading] and see about Gough's net [a boy friend]. He will be disappointed if it does not come and I should not like that.

3   I–2

Above all do not think of sending mine before his is ready, for that would seem as if I took more trouble about my own than his.

What is perhaps the earliest of these baby letters (the first to his sister) deserves to be quoted in full and set beside the very last entry in his Diary, for it shews the child of nine moved by the same sense of beauty and passion for exact description which marked the man of seventy. They form a fitting prologue and epilogue to his Life.

My dear Nelly,

    I have got such a pretty caterpillar. His back is covered with black spots from each of which a black hair comes out. He is like this. The top is yellow, then a line of blue, then another of yellow, then one of black. The little hump above the head is yellow with a black raised dot on each side of it. The part between that and the head is white with two pairs of black dots on each side. Is it not pretty? I have got an egg which we found on the 16th. It is white, covered with reddish brown specks. It was in a hole of a wall. Will you get a pair of the thinnest gloves you can get and send them to me; for we are obliged to wear them on Sunday going to church!!!! Ask Pum to send me one of those round tin boxes, corked. One of the boys found a Wagtail's nest building in the ditch. Today I heard a Woodwren going on with that mournful note we heard in the New Forest. Good bye, dear Pum,

Your loving Mig[1].

P.S. I made a mistake in the direction. I found such a dear little lizard today.

Dashing illustrations of all three objects accompany the letter.

Thus the prologue. Now for the epilogue:

Tuesday, September 4, 1923.

At Hampstead [in a nursing home].

S.W. light.

A very fine sunrise. All the lower part of the sky occupied by *horizontal* layers of cloud, through which, as the sun rose, were narrow streaks of fiery gold. The sun shewed twice, and

---

[1] Mig was the pet name by which he was known from babyhood in his family.

4

then there was an ill-defined rosy fog below, merging in the whitish grey fog lower still. The sky was full of clouds—all sorts of greys, ochreous greys, etc., too soon all overcast—leaden and by 9.0 RAIN: thick. Heard from Lady Darwin at Strathpeffer.

Wednesday, September 5.
N. light, cold.

Early in the morning the sky seemed clear, except a leaden area on the eastern horizon with level top. By 6.0 the whole sky was overcast. 7–8.30 a muffled, suffused glow on the horizon was all there was of a sunrise. 11.0. The sun crept out though the air was still very thick. Heard from Parry (Chathill)[1].

He went into hospital for his final operation the next day and he wrote no more.

If Woodcote, "this dreary place," was rendered tolerable by its birds' nests, it is easy to guess what a paradise was found in Marlborough, with its sweeping downs and glorious forest—a delightful memory. He was put under the charge of Mr W. H. Macdonald, the house-master of the Mitre, "C³," and he slept in the great U dormitory of twenty-four beds, the occupants of which were one night kept awake and indignant by his un-detected imitation of a distant barking dog. No wonder that his reports note a tendency "to be impertinent to older boys"; also a "great love for natural history which threatens to interfere with his work." But they allow him to be of great promise, clear-headed and intelligent. His "composition" has already "a freedom and attempt at style which I have rarely met with in the form." There was apparently only one occasion in all his career when he did wrong, for which he received "a severe lesson which, I am sure, will have proved a most useful one." He was placed in a high form and in due course won a junior, and then a senior scholarship in 1868, for which he was rewarded by a week's moth-hunting in the New Forest. He spent two-and-a-half years in the upper sixth under Bradley whom he venerated, and Farrar whom he did not, and he ended by being

[1] Vice-Master of Trinity, *vide infra*, p. 136.

5

second in the school. Of his companions' serious pre-occupations he was somewhat contemptuous. He played very little cricket, and less fives or racquets. Later, at Cambridge in the eighties, he took to real tennis with zeal and a certain amount of success. His most constant companion in the Clare and Trinity court was Mr Arthur Tilley of King's, a kindred soul who had just come back into residence. "He is a great acquisition up here; we play tennis together, and generally lunch after it," writes Jenkinson.

Yesterday [February 24, 1883] was so lovely: Tilley and I had the Tennis Court from 4–5 and were able to go on till 5.30, it was so light; and then we saw the sunset, very quiet, with the best set of greens and plum colour.

I keep up my tennis two or three times a week [he says in 1885] and often find myself making a stroke I never did before, which is very encouraging. Yesterday I got a back-hand half volley off the side which quite astonished me.

But at school he was no athlete. He frankly hated football —"House-matches give me a head-ache"—and Sir Henry Simpkinson, his friend and rival all through until their names appeared next to each other in the Tripos list of 1876, describes him standing "in his waistcoat and trousers and white shirt-sleeves outside the squash.... with a hand gently laid on the back of the outermost player on his side."[1]

Mr Edward Meyrick, of Marlborough and Trinity, writes of him: "Intellectually he was much the ablest boy of his year; his independence and acuteness of thought were impressive, and he was very highly thought of." Another old friend, Mr Hawes Turner, who was also with him at school and college, bears unconscious witness to the truth of his master's reports. He writes:

My impression of Mig is that he never changed at all in all the time I knew him, except in the acquisition of fresh knowledge. As a boy at Marlborough he was very good-natured—

[1] Cf. *The Marlburian* of November 28, 1923.

6

more than good-natured—kind[1]. I don't think he worked particularly hard. Scholarship amused him, and he attained it. Natural history interested him even more. He was rather impish. In moments of friendly expansion he shewed a passionate interest in holiday experiences of Scilly, and a humorous respect for the "old Emperor."[2] He was very class-conscious in those days, and, as far as I can judge, always remained so. There was no change in him when he came up to Trinity, but I became aware then for the first time of his extraordinary mathematical ability.

Nearly all the points raised by Mr Turner receive confirmation from the boy's own correspondence, *e.g.* the proportion between industry and performance—"I am fifth for the fortnight notwithstanding my efforts to keep low" [to his sister in 1867]; amusement and interest in his work—"I have been learning some practical geometry and I have found out several very useful things, such as to make an equilateral and equiangular star to any number of points, and to divide a straight line into a given number of points" [to his father in 1868, *i.e.* before the flood of handbooks on the subject had risen]; zeal for the "Emperor"—"What an idea of the Emperor's to send down 100 workmen and do that; so like him; wouldn't be disobeyed by any means"[3]; but most of all, his letters declare his enthusiasm as a naturalist, many of them being entirely taken up with observations of insects, birds, and flowers.

This taste had ample scope for indulgence at Marlborough,

[1] Cf. a passage in a letter written from Malabar in 1885 by Mr F. S. Hockin: "Pardon me if I have made a mistake in your initials. It is nearly ten years since I left Marlborough, and I cannot remember whether it should be F. H. or J. H. Five times that period will not make me forget your kindness to me at M. C. or the many pleasant months spent in your study."

[2] Viz. Mr Augustus Smith who in 1834 leased the Islands from the Crown. He was first cousin to Jenkinson's father through the Pechells.

[3] This evidently refers to an incident chronicled by Froude in *Short Studies on Great Subjects*, 3rd series, and by Mr Punch in a poem (March), 1866. There was a piece of common land at Berkhampstead which the agent of a great landowner had enclosed, as being a haunt of vagabonds, and a nest for poachers. Mr Smith, who had property hard by, "instead of bringing an action, brought 150 navvies one dark night down from London. When morning came 1500 yards of iron railings were lying flat upon the ground. They were never put up again."

which boasted a flourishing Natural History Society (*alias* the Bug and Beetle Society), founded in 1864, the first in any public school and probably the best. Jenkinson began to make notes for it even before he was admitted a member. After a year's probation he writes with pride, in September, 1866:

I am in the Society now, viz. M.C.N.H.S. We have a room fitted up as a museum with the entomological, oological, and botanical, as also the geological collections in it.

And in the Christmas Report of that year he figures as head of the entomological section. But he was also prominent as an ornithologist, contributing in kind to the museum. He writes to his father at Scilly (in October, 1866):

I wish you would have a shag set up on a plain board for me to give to the museum here. They want some birds uncommonly. I should like to pay for it myself.

Membership of the N.H.S. was not all smooth sailing. The founder and president, Mr T. A. Preston, enthusiastic but not wholly judicious, was always complaining of lack of energy, and wanting to put compulsion on a purely voluntary society, with the unfortunate results which always attend untempered zeal. Jenkinson came under the lash and his *amour propre* was touched. He vents his feelings in a characteristic explosion:

Hang the baby; the caterpillar was a Death's head[1]. I have resigned all connection with the B. and B. Society. I have not time to go to the meetings, and therefore they complained openly at the last meeting of my *negligence*; so I immediately resigned. They'll miss me in the summer—no one knows anything about moths.

This was in October, 1869. But he bore no grudge against the society, and in 1871 he read a paper on the Scilly Islands, giving an account of the fauna and flora, and another in 1872, after he

---

[1] The incident can be easily imagined although the details are lost beyond recovery. It is surmised that the peccant child was his cousin, the late W. Ogilvie-Grant, who grew up to be a notable naturalist and who would have regretted as much as Jenkinson himself the loss of a fine caterpillar.

had rejoined, on shells, "desiring to offer some hints to those who intend to collect shells this year for the Stanton prize." These two papers are his earliest published work.

His love of nature did not extend to cats, then or afterwards at college or when he came to have a garden of his own—"Five fellows were swished the other day for killing a beastly cat that had killed their pigeons; don't you think it a shame? I know I should have killed it, nasty brute." His friends still remember a *battue* one night in Nevile's Court, and his Diary celebrates the immersion of a marauder in his Brookside water-butt.

On the whole, in spite of some hardship and much ill-health, his time at Marlborough was a very happy one, and he was ever loyal to the school and to the memory of school friends and of such teachers as W. H. Macdonald, A. Babington, C. M. Bull, F. E. Thompson, J. Sowerby, although he was discriminating, and marked with ineffaceable black the names of some bad masters and bad boys.

But no doubt the happiest hours of his school years were those spent at Scilly, and a few sentences from a holiday letter to his father of July, 1869, may serve as cadence to this chapter.

I staid in the Guard's Van till Newton where his Parcels became so numerous with the prospect of West. Mor. News at Plymouth that there was no room for me. I did *not* sleep much, as I wanted to watch all he did. When we reached Penzance I had a tub and breakfast.... I went on to Vingoe and we talked about the Partridge and every imaginable subject.... We had a beastly passage, heavy swell and no wind.... We sighted the Islands (I first) at 5 p.m. exact. Passage 4½ hours. Towards the end we nearly ran down a flock of Manx Shearwaters.... I went out this morning and got several moths and 2 Tern's eggs, perfectly fresh. I wish I had my blowers. The Emperor is so nice; he is going to try and get me on to Round Island to get eggs and to let me go dredging, and to leave me on Tean one day to try and get a Curlew, but there is rather a look of nasty weather, *Wind E.* I caught today two of the little moths we got among the alders at Comrie, and tonight a nice new noctua of the same general look as the one I got on the Plane-Tree.

9

Chapter II

COLLEGE DAYS

IN 1871 he won an entrance (minor) scholarship at Trinity for which he was already entered as pensioner. His performance in the examination astonished the examiners, as one of them, the late J. M. Image, told me years ago. He came into residence, with this scholarship and a school exhibition, in October, 1872, proceeding in due course to a major scholarship next year. His tutor was J. Prior, and he began his new chapter in lodgings at 36 Market Place, moving next term into college (G 6 New Court), and in 1874 to an attic in Nevile's Court (A 3), just over his friend G. W. Balfour[1]. No one was better fitted to profit by the endless opportunities for friendship and culture offered by life at Trinity, but he did not at once realize the richness of his heritage. To his father he writes (October 15):

I cannot make out much of this place: I must get settled. I am sure I shall like it. I think I shall take to shooting as my regular amusement[2]; boating, on this stinking river, is merely a course of training, and for that I don't think I should be strong enough.

Accordingly he joined the C.U.R.V.C., rising ultimately to the rank of Captain, and his target register records a very fair success with the Snider.

The Previous Examination before the days of exemptions and soft options was a real bugbear. So the Trinity scholar can write frankly:

Little-go is getting frightfully near. How the Ploughers would triumph if they could catch me! Paley is abominable "rot," to use his grandson's polite expression.

[1] The rooms he occupied as Fellow were in Nevile's Court (A 3) from 1879 till 1884 when he took up his quarters in the fine set looking down the Avenue, immediately over the Gateway.

[2] He had shot for Marlborough in his last year there.

He is equally candid about his first small University success (March, 1873):

I am equal second for the Bell, which, although I do not like it, is as good as I expected from the exams. which did not suit me in any single way. Selwyn[1] is very good at divinity which would easily pull him ahead in an exam. for sons of clergy.

It may be said once for all that he was a good examination candidate up to the limit of his physical capacity, keeping his head and never having to pause and cudgel his brains. He was *proximus* for the Porson scholarship in 1873, and highly distinguished for the Chancellor's Medals in 1876, but he never won any of the great University prizes.

Far more emotion is exhibited over an ornithological adventure in his first term:

Today [December 3, 1872], as I was coming home past a poulterer's shop I saw a bird lying among some Dunlins and Knots, which attracted my attention. I looked at it, and the man told me it was a Quail. I thought it was rather a curious one, but I went home. Presently, however, I grew restless, and set off again, and gave the man 1*s*. for it, and took it to Baker[2]. (By the bye, it came from Norfolk.) He recognized it as the Andalusian Quail, and was delighted. However, on looking at it further, he found it was very high, but said he would try. In half-an-hour he sent it back as hopeless. I have taken out the breast-bone, examined the crop, and cut off one foot and the wings. It is such a lovely bird, with wings almost exactly the colour of a wood-cock's and back to match. Flanks unlike any other bird I know. I send you two feathers from them, which look at against a dark background. The neck and head dark, mottled brown, with beautiful quadrate white spots on the side of the throat. The work of extracting the breast-bone would ordinarily have made me sick, but I feel so savage that I could do anything.

It must be added, in the interest of science, that the feathers in question recently submitted to Mr Hartest are pronounced by him to belong not to the Andalusian but to the Virginian Quail (*Colinus virginianus*).

[1] The late Dr E. C. Selwyn, Headmaster of Uppingham.
[2] The local naturalist and taxidermist.

Long afterwards, on August 30, 1896, we find him noting in his Diary: "I read Mark Pattison's *Memoirs* till 12.30 (and continued in bed till 2.0), finding them most interesting, reminding me of my own experiences as a freshman." This, I confess, is difficult to understand. There would seem to be little likeness between the somewhat limited society of Oriel in 1832 and the large atmosphere of Trinity forty years later. Still less between the awkward, shy, self-conscious youth which Mark Pattison confesses himself to have been, and the open-hearted, simple-minded creature that Jenkinson was. Perhaps he was projecting himself into Pattison's later state with his antipathy to Boards and public business, where Jenkinson was never at home.

This is the point at which it is fitting to record the impression made by him as a young student on his contemporaries. Lord Esher writes (April 6, 1924):

I fear this letter will be a disappointment. I have looked through all my old Cambridge correspondence and can find literally nothing that could serve your purpose. Jenkinson, in those days, was no letter writer. Just as he flitted into one's room with curious bird-like movement, alighting on the arm of a chair for a few moments, and then off with a dart to someone more fortunate, so his letters to me just touch the fringe of a subject, and leave it at that. From Drinkstone[1] he used to give one glimpses of his daily life, worrying about his sister's health, lamenting his perpetual headaches. And then perhaps in a few sentences telling me of his work on "potsherds from Roman ash pits at Chesterford.... My room is quite full of them, and my head and hands also." Then, another time, he had found a coin of Valentinian and was duly elated—"It is a different thing from buying one." And so on. You must realize that ours was a curious friendship. In his heart, Jenkinson was disapproving of my rather futile life, playing about, as I did, on the outskirts of serious things, much too devoted to trivial music, to sport, and dilettantism in general. I used to strongly support

[1] Drinkstone Rectory in Suffolk, the home of the Hornes, his cousins by marriage.

Edmund Gurney[1] in his wildest rushes into Opera Bouffe and dance tunes, while Jenkinson was always trying to draw me back to the classics over which he lingered with a real appreciation, and, in those days, with a rather laborious technique on the piano. When I remember how we teased him about his "bug-hunting," how we brutally—but with kindness in our hearts—tried to shock his beautifully sensitive appreciation of the whiteness of humanity, I am surprised that he put up with us. Of course, Trinity contains many mansions. In one of the sets in which he moved there was nothing to be found that jarred upon him. The mystery is that he should have cared for that other and far less admirable set of lads who were really cut off from everything for which he cared most by their Philistinism. Yet he was constantly in and out of my rooms, in Nevile's Court, meeting there men with whom you would have thought he had nothing in common. Yet he liked them, and they liked him. I will say this, that something virginal about his delightful mind always restrained the coarser spirits of his casual companions. If you will look at what Arthur Benson says about Howard Sturgis[2], and when I tell you that some of the very happiest hours Jenkinson spent at Cambridge were spent in Sturgis's rooms, where they pecked at each other, half vexatiously and quite affectionately, you will regret, as I do, that Sturgis is not still with us and able to tell you his remembrance of a charming and memorable friendship.... When I last saw Jenkinson, a very short time ago, and we wandered about the Library together, and then walked through Clare to the riverside, I thought him absolutely unchanged from what he was as an undergraduate. In appearance, in gait, in manner, in his outlook on the world, which was always to him a world full of musical sounds and intonations, he was the Jinks of our youth. It was a delightful glimpse.

Dr J. P. Postgate gives a picture of him seen from a different angle and covering a wider field:

I did not see much of Jenkinson as an undergraduate, though we were in the same year. My first recollection, in 1873, is of asking him if he, as senior classical minor scholar, would

[1] Edmund Gurney (1847–88), Fellow of Trinity, 1872, author of *The Power of Sound* (1880), best known as one of the founders of the Society for Psychical Research. Cf. *Dict. Nat. Biogr. s.v.*

[2] Cf. A. C. Benson, *Memories and Friends* (1924), pp. 265–296. Howard Sturgis died in 1919.

join in calling on the minor scholars of the year below. He did not think this necessary.

His lack of physical robustness and his discursive interests—entomology, botany, archaeology, music—interfered considerably with his classical reading (he did not go much to lectures) and with his success in University examinations. He was three times in the final select lists (unpublished) for the Craven and other University scholarships, the standard for which, owing to the paucity of scholarships, was higher in those days than now; but he did not succeed in obtaining one. The Tripos examiners were very favourably impressed by the quality of his work in the examination, but found the quantity deficient. One of them observed privately to a friend of mine that "Jenkinson's style was admirable but his ignorance amazing!" A beautiful translation into Latin elegiacs of a famous poem of Blake, "How sweet I roamed from field to field,"[1] won especial admiration from his examiners. He was a facile and rapid composer, generally finishing early, but he soon became exhausted and was unequal to the heavy work of revising his first draft. I remember his telling me after a Greek prose paper (I think in the Fellowship Examination)[2] how it had fatigued him to think of the exact Greek word ($\dot{\epsilon}\xi\dot{\iota}\tau\eta\lambda os$ it was) needed to express the original. He was a great favourite of H. A. J. Munro, who was attracted by the finish of his literary work, and no doubt to some extent by his beautiful handwriting.

Latin was more congenial to Jenkinson than Greek, though I think he fancied himself as a composer of Greek prose. Latin appealed more to his severity of taste and his aristocratic turn of mind. The severity had no touch of austerity in it (he was a great admirer of Keats), nor of intolerance. I remember asking if he did not mind the outbursts of one whose uncertain temper was often a great trial to his friends. Jenkinson said, "No," and he added, "He is so very penitent afterwards."

---

[1] By a curious coincidence a setting of this very poem by Dr Alan Gray was given by the Trinity choir at a College feast within a month of Jenkinson's death, the front page of the *menu* being a reproduction of the translator's portrait by Sargent. J. P. P.

[2] The examination was everything in those days and the dissertations counted for little. They had already, since 1876, begun to be used as a test, but they had nothing like the weight now attached to them. I have found a paper of twenty-four pages on the character of Tiberius as drawn by Tacitus and Dean Merivale, beautifully written out and dated August, 1878. This is without doubt Jenkinson's Fellowship thesis, and a very slight affair

In matters of taste he was almost infallible, but extraordinarily difficult to please or satisfy. His was the instinctive fastidiousness of the artist, not the nice discrimination of the critic. This greatly restricted his activities and output. He was aware that it interfered with his power of origination. Of a brilliant *aperçu* of Professor Ridgeway he once said to me, "Why can't I think of these things?" He was better in private teaching than in formal lecturing. He lacked the driving power and the tolerance of half-truths which are required for the rough work of everyday instruction. Things out of the common had a fascination for him. Anything that he took up always interested him most keenly[1], and it never occurred to him that others could have a less interest in it. He once began an edition of a speech of Cicero, but soon dropped it, as he could not make up his mind on what points he should comment, and Cicero's vague phrases, which he yearned to translate with impossible precision, troubled him sorely. Of the *Hisperica Famina*[2] he made a notable edition, in extricating which his minute and scrupulous accuracy, his ingenuity and his antiquarian tastes found their proper field. Teaching, I think, had become rather distasteful to him when, to the relief of his friends, he was elected University Librarian[3].

To Mr J. A. Fuller-Maitland I owe the following note:

Though it was not I, but Rowe[4], who was Jenkinson's pianist "by special appointment," yet I got not a few opportunities of

---

it is, effective enough as a criticism of Merivale, but hardly advancing our knowledge of Tacitus.

[1] Ridgeway was once robbed of a very rare and beautiful silver coin. Jenkinson, speaking of the loss, said to me, "I think it would have killed me." J. P. P.

[2] *Vide infra*, pp. 93 ff.

[3] He had some expectation of being given a Side at Trinity, for he writes to his sister in October, 1884: "I think it very likely that if I stay in college, it may come to me to be Tutor in a very short time. If so, my present view is that I ought to take it, and that I could do it well." It is certain he would have "done it well." What better guide and mentor could a young man have had?

[4] This was R. C. Rowe who was Third Wrangler in 1877, and elected to a Fellowship at Trinity together with Jenkinson in 1878, and who died tragically in 1884 at the age of thirty. Rowe was a pianist of supreme excellence. A notice of him by Sedley Taylor in the *Cambridge Review* contains words which will recall to those who remember it the marvel of his performance.

"The possession of hands which, though unusually small, were at once playing to him, and the kind of control he exercised mainly by the expression of his wonderfully mobile face was of great value in keeping my taste in order. The influence of Cambridge when I went up in 1875 was almost entirely in the direction of a quite commendable eclecticism, which could not but dazzle one who was brought up in the strait way of the classics; the world of music seemed suddenly spread out before one, and new merits and beauties were constantly being revealed in unexpected places. It was good that this should be counteracted, and it was Jenkinson's influence, so quietly, often mutely exerted, that kept the narrow path of the highest music constantly in my view. When the *Clavierstücke* of Brahms came out (op. 76) a good many of them were beyond my powers of interpretation, and I am afraid, in spite of Jenkinson's encouragement, it was years after I left Cambridge that I mastered some of his favourites among them; he could hardly have heard them actually played, for I do not think Rowe ever took them to his heart, and it must have been with the eye that Jenkinson discerned their power[1].

flexible and firm, enabled Rowe to surmount with ease difficulties of execution which others struggled against in vain. His touch in passages of sustained expression was beautifully round and full; while in those of force and agitation it had the utmost sonorousness, vigour, and brilliancy, without a trace of the metallic clangour which too frequently mars those qualities. His power of playing extremely difficult music at first sight was such as I have never seen equalled, and I shall not easily forget how, during an exceptionally striking exercise of it, Professor Joachim pointed an admiring fore-finger in the direction of Rowe's back, while his countenance assumed an unmistakeable expression of mingled delight and astonishment.

Far above these excellences, extraordinary though they were, are to be ranked the appreciation which Rowe brought to the study of great works, and the perfection with which he reproduced them. In a melody of Schumann one heard "*quel canto che nell' anima si sente*"; in a strain of Bach or Handel, the deepest utterance of religious fervour. At such moments the whole man was absorbed by one desire—to bring out the composer's intention in its pristine integrity. To sit by his side while he thus set forth some difficult orchestral work, say by his much-loved composer Brahms, was to me a better lesson than even to be present at its performance by a full orchestra."

Jenkinson was one of those who most often thus sat by his side. He was perhaps his nearest friend and was an executor under his will; and when, announcing his death in a letter to Miss Jenkinson, he simply said, "It will make a hole in my existence, won't it?" he was using a restraint that hid a deep emotion.

[1] Mr Maitland is, I think, mistaken about the *Clavierstücke*. Rowe played them all, and especially the "Capriccio in C major," constantly, and as no one else except Brahms himself could do, and ever afterwards whenever Jenkinson opened the volume containing it he would say, "Do you remember Rowe?"

I shall never forget how, one night in the Great Court of Trinity, he stopped our (probably flippant) conversation with his finger on his lip; some of us, I have no doubt, thought he was reproving the style of our talk, and indeed, one will never forget occasions where some quiet reproof or look of disapproval made one determine never to utter unseemly words in his presence again. This time, he was not chiding us, but trying to get us to listen to a sound he could hear though most of us could not, a flight of wild geese passing far above our heads[1].

I had many searchings of heart when he admitted me to his intimacy, for with my strict Evangelical upbringing I was a good deal perturbed when he told me he had no religious belief. Not that his was the kind of militant atheism that was fashionable in Cambridge about that time; but here was a man whose life and example could be recognized as approaching very near the Christian ideal, yet who professed no personal Christianity. Were it not better, one felt, to follow such a man, even if it involved giving up all one had held most sacred? I think I soon realized that the wonderful purity, sympathy and grace of his character could never have been there without the influence of Christ's religion through past generations.

The theme announced in Mr Fuller-Maitland's closing paragraph is developed by Dr Edward Lyttelton (May 2, 1925):

I greatly enjoyed a talk with you about the "carum caput" F. J. H. J., though on thinking over what you told me I have felt ashamed at the poverty and tenuity of an estimate of him which is in the hands of the printer at this very minute and which it is too late to enlarge[2]. Your words about his approximation to moral and intellectual perfection for a moment struck me as an exaggeration; but the more I reflect on the memory he left behind him, the truer I find them to be.

It is true we appreciated him negatively; in a purblind fashion somehow discerning that there was one among us to whom all that was coarse, all that was petty and egoistic and uncomely, was not so much distasteful as wholly strange and unknown: a region the existence of which he intuitively knew but had never in the uncurbed years of boyhood dreamt of exploring. Many of us were passing through a stage of readiness to criticize others as irresponsive to a higher life, or dull to the message of religion: but I cannot remember that the most arrogant and

---

[1] *Vide infra*, p. 64.   [2] Cf. *Memories and Hopes* (1925), p. 62.

priggish ever dared to hint at any element of baseness or triviality either in his conduct or in his mind.

I am writing of long years ago. His unremitting pursuit and enjoyment of Beauty, his self-committal to the Divine Revelation which came to his untarnished heart through literature, in the spell of language, in the rich glories of the animal and insect world, made it difficult, perhaps impossible, for him to "keep up" with old friends from whom he was sundered. His vocation was not to pilot youngsters through perplexities and snares, either moral or spiritual, the very existence of which was by his child-heart unsuspected: but rather to witness to the abiding growing vision of Heaven on earth, which at that time was hidden from our callow minds. So he wrote me no letters; he could not understand our wrestlings on the pilgrimage, our deviations, our halting dismay: yet he never forgot his friends; a casual meeting would remind us in a moment of his abiding affection.

Of course to those of us who were allowed to catch a first-hand glimpse—only a glimpse—of the divine succour through struggles with infirmity, self-deceit and the turbid and tangled elements in human life, it was a regret that he did not seem to draw inspiration from the story of the Man of Nazareth. But later on we were shewn what Jenkinson's life was. It was an unhesitating, an unstinted, response to the august demand of our Master, that we are to "forget ourselves." Our friend, all unwittingly as it seemed, with an innate shrinking from all that was paltry, all self-display, all self-regard, made the great surrender to the highest and purest Thing, which through the twin channels of Beauty and Knowledge he was permitted to see. He walked among us as a child of Light.

Lord Esher speaks of a memorable friendship severed by death; Dr Lyttelton of paths divergent. There are still some left both of Jenkinson's strict contemporaries (though their ranks are dwindling), and of men younger than himself yet privileged to have a place in his heart, who either because they were his neighbours, or were like minded, or at least followed the same pursuits, never lost touch with him. If I name here Dr Lionel Cust, it is because he was the first, and not the least intimate of that select company of younger brothers who look back to moments spent with Jenkinson as the happiest and most profitable they have known or could desire to know.

Chapter III

FELLOWSHIP AND MARRIAGE

AFTER the Tripos Jenkinson proceeded to read for a Fellowship which he won at the third attempt together with J. P. Postgate, G. C. Macaulay (the other Trinity First Class Classics of '76), R. C. Rowe, G. E. Heathcote, H. Poynting and W. Aldis Wright—the last named being greatly senior and elected under a different title.

A letter of October 29 describes a pleasant interlude and gives us an amusing picture of his first essay as teacher:

Shelford, Oct. 29 [1876].

My dear Nelly,

Don't you wonder where I am writing from? Yesterday afternoon, as I was sitting in my room, our old Colonel, Wale, came in and suggested that change of air till Monday might do my cold good, which was in truth of a most violent and intractable nature. So at $\frac{1}{2}$ past 3 I arrived at the Red Lion in Petty Cury, and he drove me out 5 miles to here, where he welcomed me with five daughters, who are very nice, and some, I don't know how many, musical. It is a charming change, for, besides the comfort of the house, I look across a lawn to a park-like field or two, such as Cambridge knows not. Isn't it kind of him? But I have other news. Although my tutor has deserted me in the most dastardly manner, and not sent me one pupil, and I trusting to him lost other chances, I have had a highly interesting windfall, or rather two, viz. 2 Newnham young ladies to be taught Greek and Latin, which is to me great fun. How Turner would laugh and—but if you return to Ascot don't say anything. One of them is Miss Ritchie[1]: she has not yet ventured to suppress me, but I fancy it would be quite in her way, and the result would be a pitched battle.

I daresay when the novelty wears off I shall grudge the time and trouble, but now I am delighted; they so evidently mean business, and would so crow over any mistake on my part.

[1] Miss Elinor Ritchie, afterwards Mrs Herbert Paul.

I think Aunt Fanny would be rather amused at the notion of my playing the governess.

With one of these ladies classical coaching was varied with discussions on Discount, etc., which "her Arithmetic Master, who I expect is a duffer, can't make clear to her."

The leisure hours of these two years before he settled down to permanent work for his college and University—he was employed by Trinity from the moment of his Fellowship, the post of lecturer in classics following in 1881 and that of assistant tutor in 1882[1]—were absorbed by music and archaeology, although he did not entirely desert entomology and collected vigorously in vacation rambles.

Joachim, "the dear old man," began to play for the C.U.M.S. in 1876, and a vivid account of Jenkinson's first close contact with him will be found later on in this volume; R. C. Rowe was in residence most of the time, and London, with the Saturday and Monday Pops and the Crystal Palace concerts, was called in to supply the need when Cambridge failed. The chief content of his correspondence at this time is records and appreciation of what he has been hearing at St James's Hall.

Sound work for the Cambridge Antiquarian Society, which he joined in 1879, is shewn by joint reports made by Professor T. McK. Hughes and himself on diggings in a Roman refuse pit at Great Chesterford, in the garden of Trinity Hall, at Girton[2], where an important Saxon burial place was laid bare, and in St John's grounds, which yielded a rich harvest of Saxon remains. When Alma Tadema, in 1885, painted Hadrian visiting a British pottery, a theme which had suggested itself to him four years before, he introduced Jenkinson as a Roman Briton offering the emperor the work of his hands. Tadema called him "my

[1] It is a mistake to suppose that he was taken on to the staff at once. In January, 1879, the employment of Fellows, not yet appointed lecturers, to assist with the Composition classes, was regularized by the seniority. Jenkinson was already doing this work. He first appears on the lecture-list in May, 1881, as expounding Aeschylus to freshmen.

[2] Cf. *The Anglo-Saxon Cemetery at Girton College, based on the manuscript notes of the excavations made by the late F. J. H. Jenkinson, M.A.,* by E. J. Hollingworth and M. M. O'Reilly, Cambridge University Press, 1925.

best model" and was as much attracted by him as, thirty years later, the great artist was to whom we owe the portrait which serves as my frontispiece. He also spent money and time on coins, on one occasion losing his way among the various Farnhams before he ran to earth in Surrey the vendor of some British Philips of which he had got wind. Coins are the subject of two considerable communications of his published by the Society[1]. He held strong views on the management of museums, which he expressed with vigour both in conversation and on the rare occasions when he spoke in the Senate House: "The curator is there to preserve and produce objects when required, and not to teach." "The people who want to use a museum are not necessarily the best people to manage it."[2] These sentiments were founded on personal experience, for the Society's collections and library were placed under his charge for a short time until in 1884 the University took them over, housed them and appointed a Curator, his dear friend, Baron Anatole von Hügel. And he held the post of Curator in Zoology, with special entomological intention, but with general supervision of the University Museum from October, 1878, to March, 1879. But he was not destined for museum work either in zoology or antiquities. Henry Bradshaw had marked him for his own. They had been brought into touch by Hallam Tennyson in 1873, but the contact was not close and dynamic till the early 'eighties. It was then that the influence began which moulded and directed the whole of Jenkinson's intellectual growth. He was always a hero-worshipper, but of all the great men—Joachim, Henry Jackson, Grove, Hort—to whom he paid homage, none enjoyed such a meed as the Librarian. Never had master a more willing or docile disciple. Bradshaw had himself learnt much of the method by which he is famous from a gifted entomologist, G. R. Crotch of St John's[3], and now

[1] "On a Hoard of Roman Coins found at Willingham," C. A. S. *Communications*, vol. v (1883). *Nicholas Tyery's Proposals to Henry VIII for an Irish Coinage*, C. A. S. Octavo publications, vol. XXII (1886), this last in collaboration with G. O. White Cooper.
[2] Cf. *Cambridge University Reporter* for 1920/21, p. 692; 1921/22, p. 710.
[3] Cf. G. W. Prothero's *Memoir*, pp. 89, 90, 102.

here was a young man endowed with the same qualities of acute observation, uncommon visual memory, and scientific method, enhanced by first-class scholarship, which it was well worth while engaging in the interest of bibliography. Jenkinson had always been fond of books and had poked about in second-hand shops at Reading. There was too a certain bibliographical tradition in his family centring round the romantic figure of Sir Robert Gordon, Gentleman of the Bedchamber to James I and Charles I, alchemist and astrologer, who formed the Gordonstoun library between 1610 and 1650. But that collection was dispersed at the beginning of the nineteenth century. The catalogue of the sale made Jenkinson's mouth water in later years, but there is no evidence that he had studied it as a boy.

The following incident, however, shews that by 1883 the train had been fired. A correspondent in *The Antiquary* of August sent a copy of an inscription on a stone in the garden wall of a house at Hagenau, interesting as having been once inhabited by Melanchthon:

Quamvis custodem foribus consistere primis
    Romani quondam MB voluere patres,
Nunc tamen has aedes mea tantum ostendit imago.
    Defendant Christi numina magna Dei.
Notus ab arte sua dominus, mea signa libelli
    Quos studiosa legit turba vivenda gerunt.

Jenkinson, over the signature "V," wrote in the October number:

These lines may probably have accompanied a figure of Janus, denoting the printing-house of Johannes Secerius (Jean Secer), whose books, printed at Hagenau from 1523 to about 1535, bear the head or full-length figure of Janus as a typographical device. In the second line ME is a certain correction for MB, and videnda would satisfy the requirements of sense and metre in the last line.

This was surely no bad beginning; the power of putting two and two together is the promise of discovery.

I have no doubt that what started him collecting Cambridge books was a remark of Bradshaw's at the close of Mr R. Bowes's paper on Cambridge printers read to the Antiquarian Society on January 28, 1884, and afterwards issued as a Communication[1]. Bradshaw suggested the formation of a systematic collection of Cambridge-printed books, as had already been done for Oxford by Mr F. Madan. Certain it is that from this moment Jenkinson began an eager perusal of booksellers' catalogues and a feverish excitement over items caught or missed which only ceased with the exhaustion of the supply.

In August of this year (1884) Bradshaw and he journeyed to Manchester under the lure of Cornish's April catalogue lent by Mr J. P. Postgate, and they spent a long day in the shop. I saw them drive off from King's and I remember as if it were yesterday the gleam of Jenkinson's smile and the settled satisfaction on Bradshaw's face as they took their places in the hansom. He recounts the excursion in a letter to his sister of September 1:

I had a mad expedition last week with Mr Bradshaw. There was a stock of books from a very old library in Wales (Hengwrt) in the hands of a bookseller in Manchester. We were much tantalized by his catalogues, and longed to overhaul the lot. I had written a list of those we wanted most in his April catalogue, to ask him to send them for inspection; but when Bradshaw saw it, he said, "It's much simpler to go" (we had been very near going twice before). So on Tuesday afternoon we went by Bedford, dining from a basket in the train, charmingly and cheap. We spent all next day among the books, found some great treasures, and started by the 5 train. As we had been abominably shaken between Cambridge and Bedford, we said we wouldn't go that way again; so we ran on to London and slept at St Pancras. After breakfast we went to the inner sanctuary of the British Museum, where he is of course a great man, and worked all day, except lunch; caught the 5.5 from St Pancras and were back again. It was so delightful being with him, and freshened me up immensely.

In September Bradshaw and he went together to Bishop's Stortford to see the school books—"they are being disgracefully

[1] C. A. S. *Communications*, No. xxvi (vol. v, No. 4), 1886, with notes and additions by F. J.

knocked about"—and for the next two years Jenkinson haunted the University Library and Bradshaw's rooms. By August, 1885, Bradshaw is able to thank him for "a marvellously exact description" of some volume or other; in September he wants him to act in an emergency as Deputy Librarian. His rapid mastery of the secrets of the science amazed his friends, and it is no wonder that when Bradshaw fell asleep on February 10, 1886[1], a day which Jenkinson kept as religiously as a solemn *obit*, some of them—Hughes, Sedley Taylor, Stanford—urged him to stand for the vacancy. But he had already pledged his support to Robertson Smith and had begun to whip up Trinity M.A.'s to vote for him.

Disappointment is impossible where, as with Jenkinson, there is no tinge of personal ambition, but had he felt any it would have been lost in the overwhelming happiness of his engagement and marriage to Marian Wetton, a sister of his great friend Mrs C. V. Stanford. What she was to him (and to others) is best told in his own words to Mr F. Madan in January, 1888:

She had known very few men, but over girls and women she always had a wonderful ascendancy, which has done good to very many. She had the rather rare combination of intense earnestness with a keen sense of humour, and a very refined taste with great simplicity of character.

They were married on July 6, 1887, in St John's Church, Croydon, and Stanford played for them the Bridal March from *The Birds*. This has often served at other weddings since, but never was it more appropriate, for Jenkinson had a hand not only in the preparation of the Greek text for the performance of 1886, but in the incidental music. He was during its composition in brisk correspondence with Hubert Parry over details of rhythm and interpretation. Parry's letters are characteristic,

[1] Jenkinson had spent an hour with him the previous afternoon learning all about Cork printing, and he served on the jury at the inquest next day which he says, "was very trying, but gave me a feeling of satisfaction. He looks as peaceful and happy as if he was just going to open his eyes and be himself again."

full of good-humoured grumbles at his Aristarchus and of generous concession to his judgement: "I expect you to be right in every case." On one point he was firm. Jenkinson wanted melodrama for the Parabasis. Parry felt that there was neither time for him to write it nor for the Choregus to learn it, and he stood out for plain recitation. Recited it was with fine effect by Charles Platts of Trinity, but those who saw the revival of the play twenty years later, when Clive Carey chanted the new setting, could not but admit that Jenkinson was right. His solitary excursion into journalism was an account of the *Birds* music appended to J. W. Clark's critique of the performance in the *Saturday Review* of December 8, 1883.

The marriage was a radiantly happy one, but it had the seeds of tragedy. After a short visit to Northumberland, where he saw the Roman wall and began a friendship with Dr Thomas Hodgkin, he took his bride to the small house which was to be his home for nineteen years, but hers, alas! for but six months. The time was cloudless for them for they did not know that she was already hopelessly ill.

To return to the story of his mind and work: the impulse given by Bradshaw when alive and consecrated by his memory went on gathering strength and gradually claiming the best of the disciple's mind. Classical teaching, always faithfully and painfully executed, grew more and more of a burden. He was not a facile lecturer; he had no brilliant theories to keep the room suspended breathless on his words; his handling of a Latin text was too minute and delicate for duffers, and he would sometimes warn them off—"I don't think these lectures will be of any use to you." His preparation was exhaustive and exhausting to himself; "lucubration over a lacrimose peroration of the great Tully" was a weary end to many a weary day. His composition classes were a rare discipline in taste and style, most valuable to the scholar but caviare to the general, although any man with an ounce of perception could not but be moved by the skill and beauty of his "fair copies." Examining for the Tripos as he did from 1882 to 1885 (he sat up all night with

25

Archer-Hind in 1883, settling classes), and for the University Scholarships, etc., tried him desperately. The selection of passages for translation broke his heart. Under date September 26, 1888, he notes in his Diary, "Sunny day, but I spent it all hunting for pieces to set. It seems to get worse every time. Pure obliteration of life." He also worked by fits and starts at an edition of Plato's *Apology*, undertaken for Messrs Macmillan, which never got beyond ch. xx.

On the other hand bibliography and work in and for the University Library were pleasure and refreshment. He was an assiduous member of the Library Syndicate from March, 1886, onwards, and all that year he was busy helping Mr Bowes with the facsimile issue of the three volumes of the first Cambridge Press, and Mr Christopher Wordsworth with the third fasciculus of the Cambridge *Sarum Breviary*. Both of these tasks were legacies from Bradshaw, who in the summer before he died had made notes establishing the chronology of John Siberch's eight books. Jenkinson put these notes into order for press and they form the introduction to the reprint of Bullock's *Oration* (1521) published by Mr Bowes in 1886 together with the *Hermathena* of Papyrius Geminus and Augustine's *De miseria vitae*. He added to our slender knowledge of Siberch by discovering in a Strasbourg *Horae* of 1490 two woodcuts almost identical with those used by Siberch, thus suggesting an unsuspected connexion between the Cambridge printer and Strasbourg. It was no doubt this piece of bibliography that caused Mr Edward Arber to address him in December, 1886, as "already a famous man respecting Cambridge books." Jenkinson himself was under no illusion as to the range of his knowledge. He writes to Mr Madan in September, 1887:

Your expectations about me are too great: I don't suppose I shall ever do more than collect small items of material for other people. For instance, all that I know of Cambridge printing to 1640 will be in Arber, vol. v, and after that I shall have nothing but a few scraps from time to time.

As to Comparative Liturgiology, the only drawback is that I know nothing about it, and don't see much prospect of beginning. M. R. James is much more likely to make something of it.

Soon I shall be allowed to help to arrange the scraps[1] in U.L.C. which will be very interesting. I hope I can identify most of the important fragments. Today I saw a Caxton Indulgence in strips. A nice little list of Canterbury library (12th century) from a MS. in U.L.C., prepared for press; has it been printed? and no doubt many more such things. A parcel of slips containing the exact measurement of 20 lines of types in Caxtons, Roods, Pynsons, Machlineas, etc.

Bradshaw had been engaged for eight years on that most thorny of problems, the description of printed Sarum Breviaries for the Cambridge edition which was being prepared by Mr F. Procter and Mr Christopher Wordsworth. Two fasciculi were published in 1879 and 1882; in 1886 there still remained the third (*Sanctorale* and *Accentuarius*), which, although Bradshaw had almost done with it, still required the final touches. These Jenkinson helped to give. He was not an expert in liturgies which had been Bradshaw's pet study; in fact his interest in them was mainly bibliographical, but, as he said, he knew exactly what Bradshaw liked, and he spared himself no trouble if thereby he could improve, even in the slightest detail, any work with which Bradshaw's name was connected. So he willingly undertook the revision of Mr Wordsworth's proofs when Bradshaw was no longer there. A long series of letters in 1886, beginning on May 16, leads off: "For goodness sake correct *Trophanarius* on p. xxv. I don't know whether it is Migne's misprint, or a sort of dittography in his MS. or a recollection of *Antiphonarius*." And again: "Anyhow you won't keep Trophanarius?" Other passages shew the most acute anxiety that Bradshaw's standard of scholarship should be maintained and, by the way, prove that he was already, at this early date in his career, a past master in Bradshaw's method, which was his own. They also afford a clear indication of his character. "He waded," says Mr Wordsworth with an exaggerated depreciation of his own work that

[1] *I.e.* Bradshaw's *reliquiae*. Two years later F. J. edited the *Collected Papers*.

27

would have touched Jenkinson, "with infinite and dogged patience through stuff which must have too often disgusted his finer sense of accuracy and his perception of what he missed and would have welcomed. Like Bradshaw he certainly had a genius for teaching and the teacher's hopefulness and patience."

I cull some sentences from various letters dealing with the Breviary:

What made me question the note on 1483, 8°. Venice, was the expression "Proper and Common of Saints," which I never heard Bradshaw use. Do you like it?...A novice would think *mattins* was the natural thing to find in a Diurnale....Have you elsewhere said what a *Diurnale* is? You know H. B.'s note, "The *Diurnale*, which contains all the Hours except Mattins, as distinguished from the *Nocturnale* which contains Mattins alone and is not represented at all among the known Sarum books, has come down to us in a unique copy of a single edition." I remember his joy when he came across and brought a *Nocturnale* (I think it was Cologne) for the first time: he had never been sure of the real existence of such a book before....

Things can only be found by looking for them, and the looking cannot be done fast at the last moment. Waiting with your eyes always open is the only way it seems to me....I have put a small paragraph on p. xcviii for your approval. But don't let it seem to be Bradshaw's....You must give *me* the list of Psalters, as although I believe it is right enough not to disgrace Bradshaw, he did not as a fact, you remember, examine more than two editions, and it is best to keep his work distinct[1]

In all this correspondence there is the constant disclaimer of esoteric knowledge:

I spent all my spare time this morning with the two sheets G and H. I don't know much about these regions. But.... [here follow suggestions for rearrangement]. I am very sorry I had no more time to spend on making this section [sheets H and I] rounder and compacter: but I should have needed much more knowledge which I have not and could not get at once.... I wish I knew more of the contents of these books and then I could help you better. It seems however that people may know a good deal and yet be very stupid, Maskell for instance.

[1] Cf. *Breviary*, fasc. iii, pp. lxxxi ff. Jenkinson also made a list of *Hymni cum notis, ib.* pp. lxxxiv ff.

His hints and corrections, too many and too technical to be recorded here, were all or nearly all incorporated in the final revise to which he added an illuminating note on the sizes of books[1]. This was a topic to which he often recurred and upon which he had a short but triumphant duel in the pages of *The Academy* in 1888 with a correspondent who knew nothing about it. Jenkinson kept a courteous tone in the controversy, but in conversation and in his private letters he did not spare folk who either talked with an air of wisdom about what they did not understand, or who failed in the smallest measure to give Bradshaw his due. Of one of these he wrote to Mr Wordsworth in 1893:

Did you see ——'s notice (some weeks ago) of Bradshaw's two unfinished papers on the *Hibernensis*? I longed to write and express my feelings; but thought it better not. What a hateful little beast he is! and some beasts are at least clever; but he is an egregious blockhead. He seems quite incapable of grasping (or at least of representing) any one fact correctly. In this case he talks about the brilliant discoveries of Stokes and MacCarthy, which have put Bradshaw's work out of date. He would be puzzled if you asked him how. (It is true Stokes has taught —— that the *Hibernensis* is not a ixth century production, but then no one except —— would have required to be taught that.) As for the identification of Cumin (and Dairinis) Bradshaw had all the Cumins written out with their dates (as of course he would) and considered their claims carefully. It is a small thing to say that no man now living knows as much about the subject as Bradshaw did.

The following extract from a letter to E. G. Duff expresses the limit of criticism of Bradshaw's method which he ever allowed himself to make:

What you say about explaining typographical anomalies by comparison of preceding editions is true and important: and when you deal with *early* books you have to allow also for the *manuscript* it may be set up from. I sometimes feel uncertain whether Bradshaw always made the necessary allowance for this source of peculiarity.

[1] Cf. *Breviary*, fasc. iii, pp. cxxi ff.

Chapter IV

DUFF AND PROCTOR

IN 1887 began a friendship, in every way admirable and characteristic, being rooted in respect for Henry Bradshaw, fostered by common scientific interests, and kept fragrant by human sympathy and affection. Once or twice in each generation there arises a man whose genius is from earliest days consecrated to the pursuit and study of the printed book. Edward Gordon Duff was one of these. He began collecting before he could read and he used to trot with his 1*d*. weekly pocket-money to the bookseller's, say, "Book, please," and go away hugging whatever scrapings of the press the shopman chose to bestow. His career, which only ended in September, 1924, was a bibliographical romance and when his accumulations of half a century were dispersed at Sotheby's in March, 1925, they fetched £8099. 13*s*. The catalogue of the sale is an illustrated epitome of English bookbinding. He came up from Cheltenham to Wadham in 1883 attracted thither by the library of which he later wrote an account for Sir T. G. Jackson's *History* of the college. While still an undergraduate he was entrusted with responsible work at the Bodleian, the compilation of a list of the *incunabula*. He worked instinctively on the lines laid down by Bradshaw whom he never met, although they exchanged letters. Eighteen months after Bradshaw's death, *i.e.* in October, 1887, Jenkinson, still smarting under his loss and having no one like-minded in Cambridge, received, through the introduction of Mr Falconer Madan, a letter from this young disciple of the dead master concerning a certain "J. H.," one of Julian Notary's partners. Jenkinson replied at once:

10 Brookside, Cambridge, October 20, 1887.
My dear Sir,
    I am only too delighted to get a letter on the subject of early printing, and I should have been still more so, if I

could have helped you. I am sorry to say I know no more of the mysterious J. H. than Bradshaw could tell us in 1867 (Camb. Antiq. *Communications*, vol. III, p. 151), viz. that he and John Barbier were Julian Notary's partners, at the sign of St Thomas; and that he is omitted in 1498 (in the folio missal). It was one of *the* things Bradshaw often alluded to as an interesting problem, and I am sure I should have known, if he had found anything out about it. If you are in Cambridge, I should like to shew you one or two puzzles of my own, but not before 1500, I fear. Or if you want collations of books in the Libraries here, I shall be glad of an excuse to look them up.

Yours sincerely, F. Jenkinson.

By the time of his next letter of a few weeks later they had met and the spark was struck. Titles of ceremony are dropped and after a few months he signs himself "your affectionate friend." From then till the end, for thirty-six years, through sickness and depression, in good report and ill, the friendship never faltered. Duff's visits to Cambridge were a great and often repeated pleasure. When the long day's work in the University or some college library was over they walked home together and Duff would delight his host with a humorous song, or an anecdote, or an imitation—he was an excellent mimic and had an inexhaustible store of Scotch stories. Once or twice they went fishing together in the Hebrides. Duff was a first-rate angler, more adroit and pertinacious than his companion who was apt to be diverted to a hundred and one distractions by the river side or on the loch. It was a lasting regret to Jenkinson that Duff, when his Liverpool home broke up in 1915, settled down to a solitary life in Oxford. "I wish we had him here where we could look after him," he used to say. He was glad to bring him into touch with a kindred spirit in the person of Sir William Osler, and was as sorry for Duff's sake as for his own when the acquaintance was cut short in 1920 by Osler's death. Duff, queer fellow as he was, had a great fund of affection which he lavished on a very few. He carefully kept all Jenkinson's letters and had most of them bound. Jenkinson, for his part, never destroyed anything; the result is a correspondence, of incomparable value scientifically, and proving to those who need proof, how rich in human interest the "dry" study of bibliography can be. On almost every point Jenkinson deferred to the opinion of the other, his junior by nearly ten years, because he admitted in him a wider range of knowledge (though in his own department, that of Netherlandish printing, the Librarian was without a rival) and because he felt that, in his own phrase, Duff seemed "to fit on to Bradshaw more closely than any living bibliographer, as we understand it." What Duff felt for Jenkinson and for Bradshaw's memory is shewn by his leaving his estate in equal moieties (subject to certain life-interests) between Oxford and Cambridge—a rare compliment from an Oxford man. How these two men worked together in the cause they had at heart is well known to all students of bibliography.

A letter to Mr F. Madan of May 15, 1888, sums up his opinion of Duff and also lifts the veil on the saddest episode of his whole life, the loss which he suffered on January 5 of this year after six months of marriage, almost to a day:

I am indeed grateful to you for sending Duff to me. Now if ever in my life I feel the need of someone in whose work I can sympathize and at least try to cooperate; and to whom my joys and excitements are intelligible. Of course I do not know enough to appreciate all his knowledge; but I soon found that of people known to me now alive he is in a class by himself. His admiration for Bradshaw is only natural in him, but it is a great comfort to me, and makes me less despondent of the world as it remains. I am glad now that he did see my wife. But I do wish he could have looked back to fruitful hours in the company of Bradshaw. Think what they would have been together. He might have drawn H. B. into formulating some of his ideas.

To Duff himself he wrote on October 28, 1907:

My dear Duff,

It seems difficult to believe that twenty years ago we were unknown to each other. At any rate I am glad it has been so long, for from the first you have been a great help to me, from the time when I was missing Bradshaw, and knew no one to whom an early printed book meant anything, continuously till now, when the tares have sprung up, and I have almost forgotten the little I ever knew, and am consequently rejoiced to be given an occasional glimpse into the higher regions of bibliography. I was delighted with your paper on Scottish armorial bindings, and astonished that you had got together so much material. (This side of the paper won't take the ink, and that always puts me off)....

He had spoken of sharing his joys and excitements with Duff. Here is a case in point (1896, May 9):

The other day I was taken to a house to look at some books: some more or less in order on shelves, etc., some in a pyramid under the roof. My companion pulled out one from the pile and said, "Here's some music." It was a Sarum *Hymni cum notis* in the original binding with 10 leaves torn out at the end. There was also an ed. 1ª of John Major *quartus sententiarum* (Paris 1509, I think): and a lovely gold binding, with early manuscript service-book fly-leaves, which *might* prove to be York! At a house in Berkshire I saw an embroidered binding (Bible 163–) lying on the piano in the drawing-room, nothing accounted of. The owner was astonished to hear it was worth anything. It is nearly as good as the day it was made. In the old manor-house close by I found a vol. of 68 tracts of 1648–49, some rarish: and a volume with fly-leaves, English homilies on vellum, having the þ commonly. I took a list of the tracts and a transcript of the MS. In my dull existence these are exciting events.

Together with Duff must be mentioned Duff's friend and continuator, Robert Proctor[1], although his connexion with Jenkinson was, alas! shorter lived. We find them in touch as early as 1891 when Proctor was still living in Oxford, and for eleven years the correspondence between them was unremitting until the day when Proctor started out alone from the Taschach hut never to return. The first contact was on Wednesday, December 16 of that year, as Jenkinson notes in his Diary: "Rogers came to say Proctor (C.C.C. Oxford) was in Library wanting xvth century things. So I went and supplied him. He

[1] Cf. the vivid Memoir by A. W. Pollard in *The Library*, New Series, vol. v, and reprinted in the volume of *Bibliographical Essays* issued in 1905 for the donors and subscribers to the Proctor Memorial Fund.

dined with me (on a rotten pheasant) and we looked at Cologne books and discussed our theories and difficulties till 12." Proctor's comment, three days later, is: "I cannot thank you sufficiently for your kindness to me the other day. I shall long remember Wednesday evening as one of the pleasantest I ever spent."

How deep was the impression made by the elder upon the younger man appears from the dedication of the tracts on early printing (1895–1897): "To Francis Jenkinson, Librarian of the University of Cambridge, this series is inscribed with respect and gratitude," and from the wedding gift of April 2, 1902, of a kind rare in modern England. Proctor, as one of Morris's trustees, was interested in Icelandic, and he offered Jenkinson the first-fruits of his studies in the form of a translation of the Vápufirthinga Saga [the tale of the Weaponfirthers] which he had specially printed by Constable and sumptuously bound for "F. J. H. J. et M. C. S. IV Non. Apr. MDCCCCII." This hawthorn epithalamy—Proctor called it *Spina alba*—with its humorous Latin preface and ingenious English verses[1], is at once a witness to the scholarship and original genius of the donor and to the versatility of the recipient. Proctor was delighted with the success of his venture and wrote:

I am glad you like the little book which I look on in a way as an I.O.U. for a debt which I can never repay. With the disposal of them [the rest of the issue] I have nothing to do, but let me suggest that if there are too many, a fire is handy and useful on occasions. The Museum might not refuse a copy if it bore an autograph. Will you give my most respectful homage and salutations to Mrs Jenkinson and thanks for her note? If the job had been any trouble at all (which it wasn't, but a lark) it would have been more than made up for by such a letter.

[1] Cf. *Memoir*, pp. xxxiii–xxxv, and the touching notice of F. J. by A. Esdaile in the Library Association Record for December, 1923.

Chapter V

THE LIBRARY, 1889–1901

IN May, 1889, William Wright, Professor of Arabic, died and it was obvious that Robertson Smith would succeed him. Mr A. W. Franks of the British Museum who happened to be in Cambridge at the time, and Professor J. H. Middleton, and Robertson Smith himself, all urged Jenkinson to stand for the coming vacancy. He consented to do so, not without demur, however, for he doubted whether he had force enough to move so big a machine. But Robertson Smith pressed him, and Henry Jackson, to whom he appealed in every crisis, gave his blessing. What finally determined him was his conviction that the Bradshaw tradition would be safer in his hands than in any other, although he recognized in his rival and intimate friend, J. W. Clark, special qualities of another sort. The contest, for which lively preparation was made in the Long Vacation—"We are rather anxious about the Library (July 30). My committee are working like mad, and I feel quite ashamed at being the cause of so much trouble"—never came to a head, for Clark withdrew in August, leaving Jenkinson in possession of the field. No one was better pleased than he when two years later "J. W." obtained the post for which he was best adapted, that of Registrary; and no one admitted more gladly his great services to the Library, whether as leader of campaigns for the Reading Room (of which more anon) or for better endowment, or by the unrivalled and faultlessly ordered collection of *Cantabrigiana* with which he enriched it at his death in 1910. It is certain that the *duello* of 1889 left no bitterness between the two men and in no way affected Jenkinson's relations to the family at Scroope House. Mrs Clark always stood among the first of his gallery of noble women.

One incident of the election did ruffle him. Just before the day a third party (not a candidate) saw fit to issue a manifesto to members of the Senate, criticizing in acrid terms, by way of warning, the management of the Library during the last two decades. This included Bradshaw's reign, and Jenkinson was furious. He fell in with the writer on his way to the Senate House to be admitted and he gave him his mind between Brookside and King's Parade. Those who ever saw this gentlest of men in wrath will not envy the person who provoked it.

In his address to the electors Jenkinson had frankly stated that while all books as books interested him the older books had most attraction for him. It was characteristic that his first day's work as Librarian (October 14) should be in the tangled garden of the Palaeontographical Society's publications, a perpetually recurrent source of vexation, *e.g.*: "I am now at Palaeontographical Society—did you ever have to tackle their monographs? I go at them every few years, as Bradshaw did before me, and gain a little ground now and then" (to Duff, January 17, 1906). And to H. T. Francis (April 3, 1902): "We are quiet at the Library: I had the pleasure of getting another volume of Palaeontographical Society ready for binding: the two last preceding defeated me. Even in this the *Directions for binding* do not agree with the signatures."

The establishment over which the new Librarian was called upon to preside for thirty-four years was very different from what it is today. The entry was at the south end of the colonnade, opposite the present History rooms. The ground floor of Scott's Building to the west served as University offices. Hancock's Building had only just been completed and was not yet in use. The lower storey of Cockerell's Building housed the Woodwardian Museum of Geology. There was no Room Θ; manuscript readers sat where the Secretary now works, in the open, for there was no door shutting them off from the Dome Room. The Librarian lived unprotected at the end of this range, among the MSS. The staff consisted of himself, two Under-Librarians, one Assistant Under-Librarian, eight assistants and seven servants.

Most of these are now deceased, but seven[1] lived to greet him, to his great happiness, on his seventieth birthday, by a letter of sympathy and goodwill.

The hands were all too few for the manipulation of what was already, though the building was so much smaller, a formidable apparatus. But the duties which devolved on the Librarian might well have daunted Hercules himself. The Syndicate a few years later (November 1, 1898), pleading for extra help, set them forth in a report of which the following excerpt, where the Librarian's hand is plainly visible, will be read with interest:

"The Librarian is expected," they say, "(1) To understand MSS. both Western and Oriental; to be able to read the hand-writing in use at different periods in Europe; to consult, and sometimes to collate MSS. for students, and generally to give advice and help in all matters connected with them.

(2) To have a wide acquaintance with printed books of all periods, in all languages, on all subjects, whether from the point of view of the scholar or the bibliographer; to know what books are in the Library, and what are wanting; to keep his eye on second-hand catalogues, and to attend sales.

(3) To be responsible for the whole practical working of the Library, and to exercise a general supervision over (*a*) the Under-librarians, (*b*) the assistants, (*c*) the servants.

(4) To deal with questions relating to the catalogues.

(5) To superintend the placing and, where necessary, the removal of books—to a certain extent.

(6) To give orders for binding books—to a certain extent.

(7) To attend all meetings of the Syndicate; to prepare their *agenda* and keep the minutes; to call Sub-syndicates together and attend their meetings, etc.

(8) To supervise the keeping of the accounts.

(9) To be responsible for the care of the fabric; to superintend repairs, etc.

(10) To deal with correspondence.

(11) To conduct exchanges with foreign Universities.

(12) To consider applications for special leave to borrow MSS. or rare printed books.

---

[1] Messrs A. S. B. Miller, Alfred Rogers, E. Burrell, George Goode, W. F. Dunn, H. J. W. Wakeling and A. Baldrey.

(13) To consider applications for leave to study in the Library.
(14) To be readily accessible to all persons who frequent the Library, and to answer questions of every kind and of very various degrees of importance."

This was a counsel of perfection, or perhaps a slight overstatement made for a special purpose, viz. the increase of the staff, especially by the provision of a Secretary and of a Curator of the Oriental MSS. But it is astonishing in how many respects Jenkinson answered the ideal of the Syndicate.

Of Oriental languages it may be said that he had a little Hebrew and forgot a little Sanskrit—Dr Postgate recalls the rapidity with which he picked up Sanskrit when they read it together under the "incomparable" Professor Cowell. He worked successfully at Hausa out of sympathy with his brother serving on the West Coast of Africa from 1897 to 1898. Of most European languages, including Russian and Polish, he had a working knowledge sufficient for bibliographical purposes. He stuck to Polish after he had dropped Russian, for the sake of H. Dziedzicki's *Notes on Mycetophilidae*. He took particular pleasure in a noble page of Spanish print, and tricks of French syntax amused him. He retained his Latin unimpaired, though he grumbled at the rustiness of his Greek. But he spoke no idiom save his own and he forwent any claim to be a linguist.

In the matter of Western MSS. he always liked to have the opinion of Dr M. R. James, but his instinct nearly always guided him to a right reading and date. He was an expert collator and rendered signal service to classical scholars all over the world. Mommsen in particular was indebted to him for help with Claudian and Gildas. "All books as books interest me," he had said (*vide supra*, p. 36). He was constantly discovering fresh treasures on the shelves of the Library and he was always ready to consider with strict impartiality claims for additions in every branch of knowledge.

His supervision of the staff was that of a father rather than of a head of a department. He had their interests deeply at heart and if as sometimes happened he had to compose a difference

circa 1892

it was done in a way that left all parties better friends than they had been before.

He watched over the Catalogue with most anxious care, knowing by heart Bradshaw's rules which have been described as "probably the most practically useful set of working rules yet issued," and being fully conscious that their application makes demands on a man's best critical and logical judgement. When a sheet of the catalogue was passing through the press he would read nothing else until he had subjected it to the most vigilant scrutiny; and no proof-reader was more acute or accurate.

He was most jealous of the welfare of his books and if he withdrew any from the open shelves it was only to save them from maltreatment. It was a real distress to him to miss a Syndicate meeting, and he railed loudly against the perversity of his headaches which too often chose a Wednesday for their attack. The minutes of the meetings in his handwriting from 1889 to 1899 and again from 1919 to 1923 are a joy to behold. He kept accounts most scrupulously[1], not only public ones, but of his private purse, as Henry Jackson noted with surprise when they went abroad together, "not guessing Jinks to be so methodical." I have, indeed, small patience with the suggestion that financial intricacies puzzled him. "Business," as such, did not interest him, but he was as competent to deal with figures as any man alive.

His care for the fabric of his beloved Library may be judged from the fact that he would rise from his bed when his subconscious mind told him there was a window left open and go down in the small hours to shut it, and from the following entry in his Diary s.d. January 24, 1892:

I with W. R. S. [Robertson Smith] to Library. Having turned on water, went with Clough to lunch at the Orchard. Message from W. R. S. "Water coming in." Rushed down, turned off main. $1\frac{1}{2}$ inches in Star Room, drenching tools, new cases, etc., and dripping hard into MS. Room. Francis, Mr Vail and Hughes: with Foyster and Harrison of Jesus. I worked for

---

[1] He notes in his Diary à propos of the balance sheet of the Antiquarian Society in 1905: "—— had arranged the accounts once more under names instead of things, and no one seemed to see the untidiness of it."

two hours with dust-pans, buckets, and mops, and got ahead of it. Tea. Rogers (told in church). Waterworks manager and his men: tapped ceiling. Home to dinner. Back. 10.30 Rogers and I left. All safe."

Despite his insularity (when he went abroad it was always in the company of intimate English friends, Sir Laurence and Lady Jones at Valescure, the Henry Jacksons at the Laacher See[1] and Cannes, and above all, the Horace Darwins in the Alps) his relations to foreign visitors and correspondents were most cordial, though there was indeed one German sent over just before the War to make a list of our *incunabula* who disgusted him by his dull and mechanical operations. He delighted to serve such men as Léopold Delisle—"multorum discipulorum magister dilectissimus,"—Paul Meyer, Mommsen—"a venerable darling"[2]—Henri Omont, Léon Dorez, Max Förster, Ehwald of Gotha, Glauning of Munich, Father Ehrle. Of the many appreciations received when he went from us none shew greater insight and sympathy than those by M. Paul Desjardins of Pontigny and Miss M. E. Kronenberg of 's-Gravenhage. M. Desjardins wrote: "De M. Jenkinson je garde une image rapide, mais une idée distincte et durable. J'admire cet air d'innocence vénérable des hommes qui se sont usés à purger la science d'erreurs et d'à peu près. Je sais aussi que ce scrupuleux était un cœur profond."

Miss Kronenberg devoted an article to his memory in *Het Boek* (vol. XII, 1923) of which I venture to quote the major part, so true does it ring. After a brief acknowledgement of general obligation and a vivid sketch of his outward appearance the writer goes on:

I worked for four days (in May, 1923) in the University Library and each day I experienced the friendly helpfulness of

[1] It was on the way home from the Laacher See in 1882 that Jenkinson heard the immortal and veracious remark addressed to Henry Jackson by the inn-keeper at Flushing: "Excuse me, Saire, but how you transpire!"

[2] He collated a Parker MS. of Gildas for Mommsen (cf. *M. H. G. Chronica minora*, vol. III, fasc. i, p. 17, etc.); and also a Trinity College MS. of Claudian's *Carmina minora* for the Berlin edition (*M. H. G. Auct. Antiquiss.* fasc. x, p. xcviii).

Mr Jenkinson who actually allowed me to stay on in the building after the usual closing hour, and spared himself no pains to procure me the loan of one unknown sixteenth century book from one of the college libraries. He kept coming up to me laden with all sorts of treasures, especially Low Country incunables, in the knowledge of which he was, as Bradshaw's disciple, especially expert. Let me give one small example of his observant eye for type. I had been busy describing a Latin service-book, a Sarum *Horae*, printed at Antwerp in 1525, and, having done with it, I returned it to him. He just looked at it and put it away. Next day he brought me a similar edition by the same Antwerp printer, dated a few years later. Before handing the book over to me he glanced through it. "Well, the type is not the same." I scrutinized it closely, as is my wont, but could see no difference from the type which I remembered from the day before. "I'm sure there is a difference; the other book had not this T." I could not remember it. By way of proof the earlier edition was fetched, and in fact there *was* a difference and a very essential one in the letter T which carried a different kind of curl. This had escaped me, though I had been minutely describing the book, but the eagle eye of Mr Jenkinson, who had only cast a cursory glance, had immediately picked it out. Such an innate gift for discerning differences of type I have never found in any incunabulist. Naturally he spoke no Dutch, but I noticed casually that he seemed to understand our written language quite well. This, however, he would not allow and he chaffed me about "that language of your's which I don't understand." Much of his extensive knowledge has gone with him to the grave; but he was generous in imparting it, and many well-known bibliographers, Proctor, Copinger, Sayle, Gaselee[1] enjoyed his help in their studies; he collected and published the work of Bradshaw, his great predecessor. Of his great amiability I had an instance at the close of his life. In September a 24mo sixteenth century book was lent by the Library Syndicate to the Koninklijke Bibliotheek for my use. Those who know how very seldom English libraries allow volumes to leave their buildings will recognize in this an exceptional indulgence. In his last letter, written while he was waiting to go into hospital for an operation, he begged me to send the list of books as soon

---

[1] The indebtedness is freely acknowledged in many prefaces and dedications. Of the late Mr Copinger's *Latin Bible* (1892) Jenkinson himself wrote in 1893, "I spent 9–12 over Copinger's slips, which really I regard as mine."

as possible; he wanted to arrange for their despatch before he went. When the books came back to Cambridge at the end of September Mr Jenkinson was no longer alive.... I like best to remember him as I saw him in the Library on the last morning of my sojourn in Cambridge, a tall delicate figure with youthful eyes set in a countenance full of animation. We had taken leave of each other when suddenly he reappeared, full of excitement, with a precious Low Country incunable which I *must* see before I went away. He stood for a moment talking with me and then he said with his bright, engaging smile, "Now I don't take leave again; we have said good-bye already, you can't do that twice." So he went away.

A vivid picture of a young book-lover's first contact with the Librarian is given by Mr H. R. Creswick of Trinity College, who writes home on February 23, 1923:

I must tell you about my "Rushworth," I found it on David's stall. It is, like most of the first volumes, dated 1659; but unlike many, was actually printed in that year. It is dedicated to Richard Cromwell, and has some pleasant plates, including a fine portrait of Charles I. I went to the University Library to see their copy, and at the door was pounced upon by an elderly gentleman who seemed greatly interested.

"Hullo! You've got a Rushworth—and in its original binding too—you see those lines—they are typical of the period. Come and have a look at our copy." He stroked it and admired it and took me to the shelf where their copy is. They have one in the same binding—but the Map and Charles I are gone. The man said, "Yes, they have been torn out, probably before we had it. It came from the Ely library that was given to us; the gift that made our library. You have a beautiful copy and the plates are delightful."

After conversation in which I learned that he had been given a part of Rushworth to do for a cooperative history when at school; "You must come and see me here, and bring some more interesting books. I can shew you some of the most interesting things. If I am busy I shall turn you out, you'll understand."

"What is your name, Sir?"

"Ask for the Librarian."

So you see, I've made a valuable friend today. He is *most* charming. I shall go and see some of those interesting things very soon.

The growth of the Library from 1889 to 1923 may be traced by those who will in the Reports of the Syndics. I do not propose to go into detail here, but there are a certain number of incidents and crises in the story which deserve to be recorded as illustrating the character of my hero.

The first two recommendations of the Syndicate in November, 1898, were, it will be remembered, the appointment of a Secretary and of a Curator of Oriental MSS. other than Chinese. The Orientalist was at hand in the person of Mr E. G. Browne of Pembroke whose handlist of the Muhammedan MSS. published within eighteen months of his appointment was the first of a series of most excellent catalogues. The Secretary had to be fetched from Edinburgh. At the discussion on the Report (December 8) Jenkinson broke a lance with a member of the Senate who deprecated the introduction of "another amateur." Jenkinson, as he notes in his Diary, rose "to vindicate the Staff from the impertinence of ——." He said:

It is unfair to the staff that Professor ——'s remarks should be printed as they were spoken without something being said about it. He talks of the proposed new officer being an additional amateur. That seems to imply that all the present staff might be so described. As I myself am perhaps the one to whom that term may most fairly be applied, I am in a position to protest against its being applied to the rest.... It is only an accident that you have not at present a person who may be said not to be a professional librarian. Fifteen years ago you had the best man in his profession in England, possibly in the whole world. Probably had there been such another standing for the post in '89 you might have got him then. But there was not. You have to take what you can get.

The Librarian was quite clear as to what he wanted, and in a letter to Duff, enquiring about one of the aspirants, he traced a picture of the Ideal Secretary:

Mr Aldis of Edinburgh Bibliographical Society, V.P., is a candidate for the new post of Secretary here: and refers us to you. He seems to be a very good man; but so do some others. Is he the sort of man to *take command* wisely as well as vigorously? ...You see he is to take rank with or next to Magnússon and

Francis. His bibliography is not necessarily a recommendation. I want him to be constantly in the Library, finding out where things are wrong or behindhand, and setting them right or moving them on. Then I want a man with *some* mechanical turn; who will at least understand what tradesmen propose to do, and have an idea whether it is right. At present I have no one in the place of this kind; the one there was retired about four years ago, because he was sick of making bricks without straw. Then of course he must be a man who can give and take; and then I am anxious as to his *extraction*. Is he a man we should all get on with? Because I don't believe a place like the Library can get on unless the staff are on good terms with each other.

Aldis rose to this high standard, and indeed above it, and Jenkinson has set on record what he was to him and to the Library. When he died, after twenty years' happy work, his chief, deeply moved, wrote the following notice in *The New Cambridge* of March 8, 1919:

HARRY GIDNEY ALDIS

On the 24th of February, the Secretary of the University Library died after four days of painful illness. Murray, Librarian of Trinity College, had passed away on the 15th, the very day on which he had hoped to be set free from his military duties and to resume the important work which had been suspended during the war. The two men resembled each other both in their personal charm and in their distinction as librarians and bibliographers. . . . In 1899 the Library Syndicate determined to appoint a Secretary, the intention being to relieve the Librarian of the routine duties which absorbed most of his time. Three competent persons independently suggested that Aldis was the right man for the place; and, although competition was invited, the selection fell upon him. It was a happy day for the Library when he entered it. He was no "new broom" in the accepted sense of the term. The memory of Henry Bradshaw was still fresh in the Library, and Aldis absorbed his principles and set himself to carry them out, with such loyalty and such understanding that it was difficult to remember that they had never met.

There was no breach of continuity; no evident change. He was careful to preserve what was valuable in the existing arrangements; and he had to reckon with the limitations imposed by (among other conditions) the topography of the site. Still, he accomplished much.

The story of these twenty years cannot be told here. The removal of the Acton Library from Shropshire, the transformation of the Woodwardian Museum into four floors of closely packed iron bookcases, and the designs for further extension, urgently needed but unfortunately still waiting to be provided, are but examples of his clearness of conception and patient elaboration of detail.

It was soon found that the Secretary, imported to undertake routine duties, was also a first-rate bibliographer. His Catalogue of Scottish books before 1700, printed by the Edinburgh Bibliographical Society, in 1904, put the study of Scottish printing on a securer basis; and he has constantly helped the work of that select society in many other ways. His small volume, *The Printed Book*, written for the Cambridge University Press series, is admirably clear and authoritative. And many writers on bibliographical subjects acknowledge gratefully their debt to him.

The Library collection of fifteenth century books specially attracted him, and he found out a good deal about them as indeed he did about most things that interested him. It was his great wish to see a short catalogue of them published, and we had made some progress with it when the war and its consequences put a stop to our work upon that as upon various other schemes.

He was never idle; and it was difficult to say what was work and what was recreation, for he was happy in both. But gardening was a special pleasure to such a lover of the open air; and perhaps still more, sailing on the Broads of his native county. He was also intensely interested in machinery and mechanical contrivances of all kinds, natural history, music, astronomy, and postage stamps.

His shrewd intelligence took a man's measure at once. Fools and bores tried his patience severely. But his innate kindness spared them the castigation they deserved, and his unfailing sense of humour consoled him for the effort.

His colleagues recognize how much they owed to his sympathy and approval, which were always forthcoming. His was a radiant spirit; and it was impossible to feel discouraged for long in his company.

Physical suffering and chronic discomfort were endured with uncomplaining courage for many years; so also was the great sorrow which fell upon him in the autumn of 1917, when his son was killed in Palestine. Utterly unselfish, he bore his own burdens and helped his neighbours unfailingly to bear theirs. May his memory, like that of Bradshaw, long continue to animate the place which he loved and served so faithfully and so well.

F. J.

This eloquent witness to the writer's self-effacement, generosity and affection, and passionate loyalty to the memory of Henry Bradshaw, has taken us far from the Syndicate's Report of 1898, which *inter alia* formulated a project for the relief of the Library by the roofing in of the eastern quadrangle so as to form a Reading Room and a book-store. Something of the kind had been mooted as far back as the 'fifties by Henry Latham, afterwards Master of Trinity Hall, and had been formally recommended in 1879 on the advice of Mr Basil Champneys, but nothing had come of it. The proposal, now renewed and sanctioned in general terms by the Senate, gave rise to a Homeric conflict, to which the pen of a Fielding could alone do justice. The architect, Mr W. C. Marshall, planned a most ingenious structure which should fit into the court without touching the ancient walls and which, accommodating some 145,000 volumes, would, when other spaces in the main building otherwise occupied came into use, have given elbow-room for a quarter of a century. It was not a final solution, but it promised the palliative for which Jenkinson was sighing. As often happens in projects for academic reform, it was not until the scheme was generally approved and well under way that objections were raised; but once raised, they went on gathering strength and finally prevailed. There were protracted discussions and many fiery fly-sheets, in which all kinds of arguments, good, bad and indifferent, were adduced for and against, the most potent perhaps being the sentimental appeal to preserve intact the "heart of the University," *i.e.* the first piece of ground it ever possessed, the gift of Nigel de Thornton in 1278. It was pertinently asked, "Why given, if not to be built upon?" But "the noes had it" by nineteen votes, when the matter came to a division on November 21, 1901.

Jenkinson did not take much part in the debates, but he contributed a closely reasoned statement on "The needs of the Library considered in relation to the eastern quadrangle scheme" (a four-page pamphlet) and two fly-sheets which after the lapse of twenty-four years have lost their sting, but whose brilliant dialectic no time can dull: here is No. 1:

The Proposed Roofing-in of the Eastern Quadrangle of the Library.

I. The scheme adopted by the Library Syndicate, unanimously except for the dissentient vote of one member added to the Syndicate after the work was practically done, has had the misfortune to rouse opposition from many quarters at once. There are those benevolent souls who wish the Library to ask for something big, and then, they say, it will get it. Would the Financial Board, with all the good will in the world, say so? And *when* should we get it? If my friends had to manage the Library, they would wish to see the improvement take place in their own time rather than, too late, under some distant successor in the future.

Professor Ridgeway seems hardly to take himself seriously; so I may be excused for declining to do so. But his statement about Professor Ewing's north wall is so elaborate a joke that it might be mistaken[1]. The wall is not a north wall, and the stain was taken over by the University from the former owners of the building.

Mr Huddleston continues to spin cobwebs, whether in Mars or Nova Persei I do not know. But I leave the Registrary to continue the correspondence[2].

Mr Wood's position I confess after much study I am unable to understand. (Whether Virgil wrote the old Eton Latin Grammar or the old Eton Latin Grammar wrote Virgil is perhaps unimportant[3].) His fly-sheet appears to be a rhetorical

[1] Against the glass roof Professor Ridgeway had urged occasional leakages in the Cavendish Laboratory, "as is evidenced by the stains on the wall. Indeed a similar stain on the north wall of Professor Ewing's own laboratory seems to indicate that that structure is not quite free from inroads of water."

[2] The Registrary (J. W. Clark) and Mr T. F. C. Huddleston of King's were in pretty hot controversy at the time.

[3] The reference is to a fly-sheet by the Rev. E. G. Wood, Vicar of St Clement's, which ended with the words: "a structure which, as I write, brings back to my mind the tag of the old *Eton Latin Grammar*: *monstrum horrendum informe ingens cui lumen ademptum est.*"

exercise. The court, it seems, is not going to be roofed in, because under the roof will be a structure to hold books and readers. No doubt the scheme is different from the former scheme. The objections to that scheme are in my opinion *not* applicable to the present proposal. The gain is very much greater, and the interference with the old building so much less as to be in-appreciable. From what point of view will the new structure be "hideous"? Will it "cover nearly the whole space," when "a passage from 9 feet to 12 feet will be left" all round it? Any "book-store," wherever placed, "must" (not necessarily "constantly") "when" and *where* "used be supplied with artificial light[1]," *unless* it is in a building specially made to receive it with many narrow windows *and a low horizon*. The Law Library *is* nearly dark. Some people think better of artificial ventilation than Mr Wood does. At any rate the "natural light and ventilation" are lamentably deficient on the ground floor, and something will have to be done even if this scheme is thrown out. As to "proof" of the need of "the reading room or the store," there are none so blind as those who won't see. Cockerell's Building, full of theological books, may suit Mr Wood: we have the word of Dr Maitland, Dr Cunningham, Dr Sharp, Mr Berry, and others that it does not suit them.

I cannot understand how, in face of so many plain denials, Mr Wood can revive the inference as to exclusion of Members of the Senate from the shelves. The inference is intrinsically absurd. A room of this size may be very convenient for *some* readers, but it could not accommodate all. And once more, who wishes to exclude them?

Mr Wood deprecates classification on the shelves, and seems to think it is overdone here. I am sure it has not been overdone in the past; and I do not think it will be overdone in the future[2]. But I would ask people to consider what gives access to the shelves its value. Not, I fancy, the pleasure of walking about; but the knowledge that books on the same subject stand together, and that by looking along the shelf, they may find books they

---

[1] "The promoters of the scheme admit that the book-store must constantly (when used) be supplied with artificial light."

[2] "In particular I believe that what is called the 'congested state' of the library proceeds in no small degree from an attempt at excessive classification. Clearly, if that is carried too far, if indeed it goes beyond the five or six great divisions of the whole library, the building would in time become so extensive as to seriously waste time in going from one part to another. Our unique library cannot be managed after the pattern of other libraries."

do not know of. If the "subject" is too large (*e.g.* Theology or History, or any other ⅛th of the whole field of human knowledge), they might as well sit still and have their books brought to them. On this point all authorities on library arrangement are against Mr Wood. I do not know in what respect our library is "unique." At any rate the congestion has nothing to do with classification.

"An independent Syndicate"![1] Independent of what? Why not an independent Council of the Senate? Or an independent Electoral Roll?

I hope no one will vote placet who wishes the scheme may be defeated[2].

"Mr Chadwick's remarks seem to indicate that there has been a certain unwillingness to consider alternatives. This too seems to me unscientific." To me also, most unscientific. Mr Chadwick as I have said only came on the Syndicate when the work was done. I cannot believe that he wishes so much importance to be attached to his late misgivings.

I know that Mr Wood loves the Library, and I hope he will never love it less. He certainly has no need to apologize for intruding into the present controversy. Such students are a part of the place, and to see them at work is the best encouragement a Librarian can have. But they do not necessarily understand the machinery of the department; and if the Library Staff are, as we have been told, amateurs, some students are still more so.

I had no intention to write so much: but I disagree with almost every word Mr Wood has written. Some will believe him: I hope a few will believe me. To those who have made up their minds long ago and are now occupied in improvising plausible excuses, I do not appeal.

November 20, 1901   F. JENKINSON.

Simultaneously with this fly-sheet there appeared a short one on the other side over the signatures of the Masters of Clare and Magdalene and six others:

In view of the Recommendations of the Financial Board contained in the issue of yesterday's *Reporter* for the purchase

---

[1] "The time has come for the appointment of an independent Syndicate to go into the whole question of the needs of the library," etc.

[2] "I am told of Members of the Senate who say they are going to vote *placet* with a heavy heart or who will do so wishing the scheme might nevertheless be defeated."

of a further portion of land from Downing College, at an estimated cost of at least £25,000, it appears to us most undesirable, while we fully recognize the claims of the Library, to proceed with the present proposals of the Syndicate. We therefore suggest that the Syndicate should not press its proposals at tomorrow's congregation, but should allow an opportunity for considering the scheme afresh under the altered circumstances created by the Recommendation.

Jenkinson replied at once with No. 2:

The Proposals of the Library Syndicate.

What has been decided by the vote today?

The refusal to allow the Vice-Chancellor to accept certain tenders cannot override the Graces of January 31 last (*Reporter*, p. 519) approving the Recommendations of the Syndicate: 1. "That a general approval be given to the plan submitted by W. C. Marshall, M.A., architect, for roofing, and adapting to Library purposes, the eastern quadrangle of the Library": and 2. "That authority be given to the Library Syndicate to obtain further details, specifications, and tenders; it being understood that the work be not undertaken without further reference to the Senate." It could not override these Graces even if the Opposition had allowed the Senate to have a plain issue before them.

This they did not do. Instead they angled for votes by issuing an ostensible appeal to the Library Syndicate. I say ostensible, because they did not think fit to communicate it to the Syndicate, which presumably they could have done, if they had wished it: especially as the ordinary meeting of the Syndicate was held at noon that same day. Votes they do seem to have caught; but they also confused the issues: so that their majority of nineteen merely declares the present time inopportune.

This inopportuneness had escaped the vigilance of the Financial Board (*sensu stricto*). But we now see what is meant by an "independent" syndicate, board, etc.

There was no opportunity for explaining to the Senate (who, we are told, have not time nor leisure to read reports) that the expenditure on the Downing site would be spread over many years; and that consequently *expenditure on the Library, if inopportune now, will be equally inopportune for some time to come..*

50

Yet the signatories are "honourable men." They *"fully recognize the claims of the Library."* If this is recognition, one may well wish to be ignored.

No doubt the *capita conjurationis* are chuckling over the simplicity of their followers: and perhaps they are justified in doing so.

1901, *November* 21. FRANCIS JENKINSON.

This Parthian shot betrays extreme irritation and impatience, and there is no doubt that Jenkinson was very angry. He wrote to his sister on November 22:

My dear Nell,

I am not composed enough to write a real letter. The voting is over (and for the time we have received a check) but the result was almost certainly due to a rather disgraceful fly-sheet sent out too late for a reply. So last night I set to work to shew it up: and the Master of Magdalene is "surprised and pained"; so I have been writing him a long letter, which ought to put things right, if he was not, as I hope he was not, responsible. If he *was*, I can't help it: I won't stand foul play from any one. But it is all very wearing.... My last fly-sheet, if it did nothing else, made Dr Sharp have "such a hearty roar of laughter as I have not enjoyed for a long time."

And to Duff the day before:

Aldis and I have had a reverse today. The Senate have chucked out the scheme for Library Extension. Poor devils, of course they know nothing about it, and are misled by a gang of plausible scribblers. They drew a very strong red herring (which no decent person would touch with a barge-pole) across the track last night. There was no time for a counter-demonstration; and I believe that really decided the issue: but *what* issue by their own action they have made uncertain. I hope we shall soon have it all up again somehow.

Jenkinson was not so angry perhaps as the Registrary, J. W. Clark, who had taken up the scheme with his usual zeal, energy, and knowledge, and had borne the brunt of the controversy with speeches and pamphlets. One of these entitled *Remarks on the Scheme*, etc., which, besides its persuasion and advocacy pertinent to the case, is a valuable piece of architectural history, illustrated by plans and elevations, commanded the respect though it could not turn the heart of his opponents. And "J's" vexation was deep and vocal. The story goes that meeting a leader of the other side on the pavement by St Mary's Church, so loud an altercation ensued that the cargo of the old horse-tram besought the driver not to move until they had done wrangling.

But the hurt took long to heal and if the Librarian came at last to forgive the *non-placets*, he always remembered them with pity.

Within twelve months of this incident the rooms occupied by the Council and Vice-Chancellor on the ground-floor of Scott's Building were restored to the Library, but were immediately requisitioned for Lord Acton's books which, having been saved from dispersion by the generosity of Mr Andrew Carnegie, were, on Acton's death in June 1902, given to Mr John Morley, who forthwith presented them to Cambridge; of which more anon.

Chapter VI

THE LIBRARY 1902–1913

THE year 1902 deserves a white stone. After his wife's death in 1888 Jenkinson went on living at 10 Brookside, not indeed unbefriended, for many doors were open to him, but solitary, save for the occasional presence of his sister, or of a sister-in-law, or of some visitor on bibliography intent. But now on April 2, 1902, light and warmth came into his loneliness by his marriage on April 2 with his dear friend and cousin *à la mode de Bretagne*, Miss Margaret Stewart. I do not propose to trespass upon sacred ground, but I am sure that all Jenkinson's friends will join in thanking her who by her watchful care and absolute sympathy of taste brought him some degree of better health and quickened, if that were possible, his zest in all things lovely and of good report. Her music especially was an unceasing joy to him. Years before this, I find praise in his Diary for her interpretation of Purcell, Rameau, and Couperin—"It is wonderful how she fetches out the poetry"—and a letter to me in 1897 sums up her style:

You must console yourself for Daisy's absence by considering how she brightens my existence. I have just been dining at the Lodge [St Catharine's] and she got started at the old piano and gave us quite a concert (improved by the extraction of a *hairpin* which lay in the piano and made a horrible whizzing). I hope it will be good for Miss Somerset [now Mrs J. O. F. Murray] to hear her, as it is just what she cannot hear any one else do. It really seems to me more wonderful every time I hear her: that distribution of expression fairly over all the notes, and nothing scamped or put in perfunctorily.

Let me give one instance of the courage with which both of them, frail in body but unconquerable in spirit, faced troubles which seem trifling in a retrospect but are great at the moment.

It was for many years their custom to keep Mozart's birthday, January 27th, with proper ceremony. In 1922 it was to be on a larger scale, in a hired hall, with a dramatic scene written for the occasion by Miss Margaret Cropper—a passage between the ghost of Mozart (Mr John Burnaby) and the Jenkinsons' small Stewart nieces. Mrs Jenkinson had besides to play in a trio and a quartet, but on the morning of the day she was in bed with a feverish cold. She said she must not disappoint her guests. The doctor refused all responsibility. "It is at your own risk. You and Mr Jenkinson must settle it between you. I repeat, I consider that at your age you are running a grave risk." She appealed to her husband who said to the doctor with a smile, "We seem very old to you, no doubt, but we don't feel old, and when you come to our age you will probably feel the same, and I rather think that the disappointment of not going would do her as much harm as to go; so I think we'll risk it." They had their way; she rose, dressed, never played better, and was not sensibly the worse for it. The doctor, who was present at the party, remarked, "You don't look like the same person I saw this morning." This pleased Jenkinson immensely and he said to his wife, "I think you triumphed there."

In October, 1902, he went to Oxford for the Bodleian ter-centenary celebration to receive together with J. W. Clark and a number of eminent librarians the degree of doctor, *honoris causa*. Traube was there and Paul Meyer who, in responding for the guests at the banquet in the hall of Christ Church, delighted the company by his wit. "Si j'avais vécu au xive siècle j'aurais sans doute parlé en anglais." Jenkinson was presented for his degree in a group with Herr von Laubmann of Munich and M. H. Omont of Paris, an especially congenial spirit who in September, 1923, wrote to me: "Les trop rares occasions qu'il m'a été données de rencontrer M. Jenkinson m'avaient fait apprécier la noblesse de son caractère et la sureté de son érudition. Quelle perte pour votre bibliothèque qu'il dirigeait en digne successeur et continuateur du regretté Henry Bradshaw! Les deux noms de les deux grands bibliothécaires resteront à jamais étroitement unis." Jenkinson, for all his modesty, would have welcomed the salutation.

The negociations, first outlined in August of this year, for the transference of Lord Acton's library from Aldenham Park to Cambridge, began to take shape about the time of the Oxford visit. On October 20, Mr John Morley, afterwards Lord Morley of Blackburn, wrote to the Duke of Devonshire, Chancellor of the University, a classical letter announcing his intention of presenting to the University the library of the late Regius Professor of Modern History. "The Acton Library," he said, "is not one of those noble and miscellaneous accumulations that have been gathered by the chances of time and taste in colleges and other places of old foundations," but "collected by Lord Acton to be the material for a history of Liberty, the emancipation of Conscience from Power, and the gradual substitution of Freedom for Force in the government of men. That guiding object gives to these sixty or seventy thousand volumes a unity that I would fain preserve by placing them where they can be kept intact and in some degree apart." Jenkinson went to lunch with the generous donor, Mr John Morley, and amazed that man of letters by the skill and rapidity with which he made a parcel of the manuscript catalogue. Some weeks later he went down into Shropshire with Aldis and began the business of sorting the books, which were in considerable confusion. They worked all day for several days and returned to Aldenham again and again during the next four months. The last of his visits, in February, 1903, when his wife accompanied him, was disastrous. Physical exhaustion rendered him then, as always, an easy prey to influenza. He notes on February 7: "Had a very bad night, identifying myself with a long set of 4° periodicals, and being much surprised as the morning came to find so much discomfort all centred in my own body. 100°–101°." This attack imprisoned him in a country inn till February 24.

He describes the situation to Duff on February 9:

I do so wish you were still at Shrewsbury, as we might have met. For although I ought to have no spare time at all, I have broken down, for the fourth time this winter, and if I go back to Aldenham tomorrow, I shall be lucky.

I am not sure whether you know that Lord Acton's library, bought by Carnegie, and on Lord Acton's death given to John Morley, was by the latter given to us—that is to say, *most* of it: and herein lies the gist of the matter. *To sort out what could best be spared* of 60 or 70,000 volumes is no joke, as you will understand, though Mr Morley assumes it is child's play. I was here twice in November, and am now here again (with my wife); also Aldis, Burrell, and Baldrey, an excellent trio for the work: and we are in sight of port, for the packers arrive tonight, and go on till they have finished. When the books are at Cambridge, we shall have enough to do. I do not think there is one book to interest you in the whole collection. There are a few xv cent., the best being *Der Stadt Worms Reformation*, 1498, a handsome book which I never saw before. I have come across nothing English earlier, I think, than Elizabeth. But I am told of a xv cent. Missal in the church here, which I mean to see if possible; and if it is in your line, will make a note of it for you. This is a charming old place; and this hotel (Crown Hotel, Bridgenorth) very quiet and comfortable.

When the main bulk of the books, over forty tons in weight, conveyed by five pantechnicon vans, reached Cambridge, the labour of cataloguing and placing them began. A special staff was constituted for the purpose under the superintendence first of Miss A. M. Cooke of Manchester University, then of Dr T. A. Walker of Peterhouse, and lastly, from 1912 to 1913, of Mr A. T. Bartholomew who had been associated with the work from the beginning to its great benefit and his own. The Librarian exercised a general control and he was particularly active in completing defective sets, of which there were a great many owing largely to Lord Acton's habit of translating into practice Grolier's motto, *Et amicorum.* But the collection, despite its inestimable value as an aid to the historical student, was hardly one after Jenkinson's heart, for among its sixty thousand volumes it contained only about sixty incunables, and less than thirty English books printed before 1640. What pleased him perhaps most of all were the slips of paper with which nearly every book bristled, marking noteworthy passages, evidence of Lord Acton's learning and personal practice.

It was ten full years before the Acton Library was finally catalogued and classified, but it was available for readers as soon as the preliminary arrangement of the books on the shelves in the west end of Scott's Building was effected.

The Library Syndicate on the completion of the long task in 1913 issued a valuable report, drafted by Sir Adolphus Ward, giving the history not only of Mr Morley's donation and the manner of its employment but of the growth of the Aldenham Library from the time of Sir John Acton (1736–1811). This amply recompensed Jenkinson for his labour.

The next event which ruffled the calm of the Library was the removal in 1905 of the Law Books to the recently built Squire Law Library. The lawyers, naturally anxious to equip their shelves with the least possible expense, prevailed upon the Library Syndicate to recommend that duplicates and books of solely legal interest should be deposited with them in Downing Street.

Seven Syndics, including Dr Henry Jackson, Dr M. R. James, Mr N. McLean and Mr R. V. Laurence withheld their signatures, and Jackson was vigorous and uncompromising by speech and pamphlet in his opposition to a scheme which involved, as he believed, the destruction of books, to be "hacked by students preparing for Triposes," the beginning of the disruption of the Library, and the violation of a trust. Mr Laurence as a historian deprecated the divorce of books on law from books of history and political philosophy. Even Byles on Bills, he remarked, might come to have an interest to others besides professional lawyers.

The Grace sanctioning the proposal was non-placeted, but carried by a majority of 17 in a house of 143.

Jenkinson did not express himself in public on this topic, but I have no doubt that he stood with Jackson, for he was, as we shall see, extremely sensitive in the matter of copyright; he disliked decentralization on principle, and doubtless foresaw difficulties and complications of administration. I surmise that his lips were sealed by the contrary advocacy of F. W. Maitland, a man for whom he had a veneration almost equal to that which he felt for Henry Jackson.

The year 1905 was fraught with great happenings. First there was the Library Appeal. On the one hand, the increase of space at the disposal of the Librarian, who had now entered into possession of all the buildings abutting on the two quadrangles and needing to be adapted to library purposes; on the other hand, the incessant increase in the number of books, besides the recently acquired Acton-Morley collection, clamouring to be housed and placed; the want of more hands to deal with them, and of modern appliances, such as telephone and electric light for the facilitation of their task—all this meant a capital sum of about half a million, which it would be fantastic to expect from the University Chest. Accordingly an appeal to the public, over the signatures of the Vice-Chancellor (Dr Chase), the Librarian, and the Registry (who was its real initiator and most active promoter), was issued by the University Association with the approval of the Library Syndicate. This appeal, a nine-page pamphlet which went through five editions in as many years, netted £20,000, approximately the amount required for immediate necessity. It was launched at a meeting in Peterhouse Combination Room on January 24, and to the Librarian fell the duty of moving the first resolution, viz. "that exceptional measures are necessary in order to make the organisation of the University Library more efficient and more worthy of the University." This he did in a speech which he himself described as scrappy but which is so rare and so important an expression of his mind on his life's business that it must be given *in toto*:

After the statement you have heard from Mr Clark it appears to me to be less necessary than ever that I should say very much. He has put before you a condensed view of the Appeal which is in print, and has really said all that need be said. At the same time there are a few things relating to particular details which I may perhaps advantageously say.

It is impossible in a few minutes to present a picture of such an organisation as that to which this motion refers when it says: "to make the organisation of the University Library more efficient and more worthy of the University." That is a very general expression, and it seems to me that, in some respects, I am hardly the person to propose this resolution. But the organisation of the University Library covers several things with which I am of necessity more familiar than most members of the Senate. I shall not fear contradiction when I state that the various departments are constantly growing, and tending to become too large to be directed efficiently by the persons who have them in charge, managing them single-handed, or, as the case may be, two together. Therefore, we want more members of the staff among whom these different departments may be divided. This whole question is affected by the fact that all this work has to be done in public. We have no seclusion in which we can devote ourselves to finishing off whatever most needs to be finished; and working in public, we are liable to constant interruption. Work conducted under such conditions is far from economical.

In some cases it is desirable to concentrate in one officer duties now partially discharged, if at all, by several.

The time has come when all the binding should be superintended by one person, whose time would be fully taken up in seeing that the binding and rebinding is properly done.

The General Catalogue, again, should be a separate department by itself, entirely in the charge of one person. I shall return to this question presently. But first let me say a word on the subject of cataloguing. As far as current literature is concerned, the work is done promptly and completely, by the two Under-Librarians and two or more Assistants. The time which they can spare from this work is devoted to recataloguing books which are at present recorded in the old catalogue only; and also to cataloguing special collections which from time to time come to the Library either by gift or purchase. This work is always proceeding, but it never has been cleared off, and never will be until more hands can be set to work upon it. It must, however, be borne in mind that, even if we could catalogue faster, other obstacles have hitherto stood in our way. Before a book can be catalogued it must be placed. Perhaps in the future this may become possible; in the past it has been impossible. We have had thousands of books for which no place could be found upon the shelves; and hundreds, or I think I may again say thousands, which required binding. It is impossible to catalogue books until they are placed, and it is very undesirable to catalogue them until they are bound, because if they are catalogued they have to be used, and if they are not bound they cannot be used without damage to themselves and annoyance to the person who uses them.

Again, cataloguing old books is much more difficult than cataloguing new ones. That is a thing which is very often forgotten. It is no use to say: "You ought to do double the amount; go faster." Twenty-five years ago, in response I suppose to external pressure, the work was hurried on at an enormous pace; for several years about four times as much was done as it was possible to do properly; and I think I may say that we are still suffering from the results, because hasty cataloguing is not merely work that is indifferent in itself, but it sets things in a wrong direction. Precedents are established and it takes years to eliminate the effects of work which has not been done thoroughly and carefully.

I said just now that the Catalogue should be supervised by one person. I meant by this that there should be a person in charge of the Catalogue entirely irrespective of current cataloguing work. The Catalogue requires constant revision in order to secure uniformity and lucid order. I am sure everybody here who uses the Catalogue knows perfectly well that there is room for improvement. The larger articles require, if you take them collectively, continual revision. There is work enough there to occupy all the time of one Under-Librarian and one Assistant. By the time he has worked through the whole Catalogue, it is time for him to begin again.

This brings me to a point which I particularly wish to urge upon you; and that is that we badly want a second copy of the Catalogue. It is exceedingly rash for us to go on as we are doing at present with only one copy of this enormous index to the Library, in which, if a title-slip is lost, there is no way of detecting its absence. A second copy is needed for three reasons: (1) as a security against loss of slips from the single copy exposed for public use; (2) to be used by the cataloguing staff in comparative seclusion and freedom from interruption; and (3) to enable rearrangements of these large headings and of whole volumes to take place without withdrawing them from the use of readers and staff alike.

In the next place we have to consider what the cost of a

second copy of the Catalogue would be. 440 volumes at 30*s.*
amount to £660. This sum need not be all spent at once, but
still it is initial expenditure. Then there must be the proverbial
"man and a boy," who must employ the whole of their time in
cutting out the titles (which are printed in sheets) and pasting
them in in proper order, under a certain amount also of first-
class supervision. I have a note of the total number of titles
that have been printed for the General Catalogue since its beginning in 1861: there are 300,000 odd, besides secondary
entries and slips with written headings; in all 375,000 slips to
be pasted in the second copy of the Catalogue. This will mean
something like £100 a year, or more, for several years before
the second copy could be completed; and the longer it is put off
the more expensive it will be.

I wish to say a few words on one other point, and that is upon
the money needed to enable us to acquire books. The Vice-
Chancellor said that people fancy we get all the books we want
under the Copyright Act. Well, in the first place it must be
remembered that we have to claim those books, and that is a
very heavy duty upon us. I gladly record the fact that many
publishers send their books spontaneously, but some do not.

When we have succeeded in acquiring our supply of copyright
books, our work is not done. They form a nucleus to which, it
seems to me, we are bound to spend every penny we can in
adding other books, both old and new. New books are produced not only in Europe, not only in America, but in India,
in some of our Colonies, and even in the extreme East. We
want a very large sum to spend upon modern books alone, and
also upon periodicals. Our foreign current periodicals number
1,400. Some of them are given, a great many of them are
bought; and I think we want at least half as many again if we
could afford to buy them.

Besides new books there are old books. We ought to take our
share in retaining old and valuable books which turn up now and
again, and placing them where students who want them can
find them. From this point of view it does not matter whether
they go out of the country or into a private collection; they are
lost sight of, or at any rate are inaccessible. We cannot hope now
to buy a Mazarine Bible, or books printed by Caxton, or
Shakespeare quartos; but we can recognize that if there had been
more intelligent foresight and more interest taken in the Library
in the eighteenth century all those things might have been here,

and might then have been had for small prices. Much more was done at Oxford, not entirely because there was more money there. Oxford men have always taken the Bodleian Library seriously; Cambridge men, as a rule, have not taken the University Library seriously. In the index to the *Annals of the Bodleian Library* I find that the word "theft" does not occur. If we had a history of the Cambridge Library in the seventeenth and eighteenth centuries it would occupy, I suppose, half a column; for books are said to have gone away in those days in cartloads. But though we cannot undo the mischief done by the indifference of our predecessors, we can, by even moderate expenditure, skilfully directed, save ourselves from being reproached by our successors. An intelligent anticipation of rises in value brings a sure reward. While rich collectors are hunting for the books that have already become expensive, we can be selecting the books which have not gone up yet, but which will go up most certainly. Something in that way has been done already. We have abundance of expert advice in Cambridge, and all we want is money. Expert advice is useless without the means of acting upon it. It is most mortifying to have people come to us and say: "You ought certainly to buy this book"; and to be obliged to answer: "We have no money to buy it with." That is our experience almost every week.

I may give one instance, in which, it is true, a rather large sum is required. The literature of Buddhism is, and ought to be, a subject of serious study at Cambridge. One of our great wants has always been the Tibetan translation of all the Sanskrit texts. This version, being very ancient and absolutely literal, occupies a position like that of Aquila's Greek version of the Hebrew Bible. Berlin possesses, I believe, the only complete copy in Europe. Another, as a member of the Senate has recently ascertained, is now to be had, in the far East, for about £1,400[1].

I have been unable to do more than indicate a few points in which our organisation, to be effective, needs "exceptional measures." But I hope I have said enough to justify my position as proposer of the resolution which has been read to you.

In August, 1905, came the visit of the Library Association. Naturally his mind was full of the former meeting at Cambridge in 1882 when Bradshaw had presided and had given them of

[1] This want was shortly supplied through the munificence of Dr C. Taylor. *Vide infra*, p. 85, n. 1.

his best. Jenkinson's Address as President, composed with much heart-searching and at high pressure—it was only finished at 1.30 a.m. the day before its delivery—was chiefly devoted to telling what Bradshaw had done for the collection of fifteenth-century books in the University Library; but it also contained discursive remarks on the treatment of books in general. He took occasion to air some of his pet grievances, *e.g.* the badness of modern paper (he once dropped subscribing to an otherwise meritorious journal because it was printed on "stuff which it is a misery to handle"); the mischief wrought by the binder's machine which splits every leaf half an inch up the back. ("Rebinding will not undo it. If you mend every pair of leaves, you will have a lump like an onion at the bottom of your book"); the insufficient packing and protection of books sent by post or rail. "The care of books is a difficult business. Reforms are wanted in the books and in those who use them." An eloquent passage justified his love of old books:

In these days when printing, like the decorative arts, is so sadly and monotonously spiritless and mechanical, the sight of these early books, which shew freedom and style in type-cutting and in ornamentation, substance and surface in the paper, and lustrous blackness in the ink, may help to remind people that books were not always what most of them are now. And for the bibliographer, whom it is one of the objects of the Association to encourage and to educate; where can he learn his work so well? The man who can collate an early book without signatures, with quires of varying size, cancels, and other obstacles to be surmounted, will think nothing of the structural difficulties of later books: whereas if he begins with later books, in which structural peculiarities are much less common, he is apt to overlook such things altogether when he comes across them.

He closed with two personal anecdotes: (1) how he recovered in 1899 some missing leaves of Etienne Poncher's *Decreta Synodalia* (1515) and (2) how he had recently missed the Costerian *Doctrinale*. The happy ending of this last story is related later in this volume[1].

[1] *Vide infra,* pp. 85 ff.

63

He had begun his Address with an apology for its matter and style:

It is now my business to deliver to you some opening remarks which in the formal programme are dignified by the name of the Presidential Address. It will not be the kind of Presidential Address you are accustomed to listen to, but I have written down a certain amount which I will now utter.

But Dr Thomas Hodgkin expressed the mind of all present when he thanked the speaker for enlarging on the difficulties and romance of book-collecting, and for the outpouring of a pure heart in tribute to Henry Bradshaw by one who was carrying on in the same spirit the same enrichment of the Library entrusted to his care. Jenkinson was more than pleased by this.

Two days later he and his wife gave a garden party (an anxious undertaking) in the Trinity Roundabout, and in the evening there was a dinner in the hall of King's, when Mr Sedley Taylor paid a deserved compliment to the President for the way in which he had conducted proceedings. "The late Mr Cecil Rhodes," he remarked, "used to say that Fellows of Colleges knew nothing about business. If Mr Rhodes had been taking part in the Conference during the last few days, he would have thought differently. But perhaps Mr Rhodes after all was only speaking of Oxford Fellows."

A tired man was Jenkinson that night. The day after, his Diary chronicles excitement of a different kind:

August 25, 9–10 p.m. Great movement of redshanks. For a long time there was no other note: then dunlin (if not curlew and sandpiper) rarely, ring-plover (once or twice) and once, I am sure, spotted redshank (my father has often whistled the note). 10.30. Curlews in large numbers. Note like dunlin but prolonged into two. Spotted redshanks again, and one or two sounds I could not identify. ? Greenshanks.

While I have this year's Diary open, I cannot refrain from transcribing a passage which is neither bibliographical nor scientific, but simply aesthetic. He is in Morayshire for his well-deserved holiday and notes, *s.d.* September 16: "At Dunphail station the H— family got out, three or four girls in kilts, their hair in fringes and pigtails—a disgusting spectacle."

In 1907 Mr Magnússon, the Scandinavian scholar, retired after thirty-eight years' service, and Mr E. J. Thomas, whose erudition was a constant comfort and delight to Jenkinson, became Under-Librarian.

In 1910 Charles Sayle was appointed Assistant Under-Librarian, having been associated with the Library in one capacity or another since 1893. He survived his beloved chief by nine months, and it is no secret that it was he who wrote the touching and reverent obituary notice of Jenkinson in the *Times* of September 22, 1923. On Sayle's death in July, 1924 (which followed close on that of another faithful friend, Mr H. T. Francis), a mass of notes and *obiter scripta* were found in his rooms, collected mainly with a view to that notice, but going far beyond its limits in a sedulous preservation of every scrap of information which should remind him of his master. Sayle's pen was seldom still, but the work by which he will be chiefly remembered is his *Catalogue of Early English Printed Books* (four vols. 1900–1907) undertaken at Jenkinson's instance[1].

When F. W. Maitland died, universally regretted, at Grand Canary in December, 1906, Jenkinson was summoned to fill his place as Sandars Lecturer. The Sandars Lecture, the first English endowment of bibliography, was founded by a great benefactor to the Library concerning whom Jenkinson wrote:

Samuel Sandars, M.A., of Trinity College, appears among the donors of books as far back as the year 1870: and from that time onward his watchful generosity has again and again relieved the anxiety of successive librarians by securing, or enabling them to secure, specially desirable books which but for his help would have been lost. Latterly it was his habit to entrust to the Librarian

[1] A most graceful and convincing appreciation of Sayle was written by the late Master of Magdalene in *The Cambridge Review* of October 17, 1924 (reprinted in *The Library*, December, 1924).

a sum of money to be spent at his discretion, thus supplementing the diminished income of the Rustat Fund[1].

By his will Mr Sandars left to the Library a valuable collection of MSS. and books (many printed on vellum), money to buy others, and also £2000 to endow an annual or biennial lectureship on Bibliography, Palaeography, Typography, Bookbinding, Book Illustration, the Science of Books and Manuscripts, and the arts relating thereto. The only conditions laid upon the lecturer are that his work is to be founded on and illustrated by examples contained in the U. L. C. or in college libraries, and that before receiving payment he shall deliver a written or printed copy of each lecture to the University Library and to the British Museum.

The electors are the Vice-Chancellor, the Master of Trinity, and the Library Syndicate. The series was inaugurated in 1895 by Sir Edward Maunde Thompson, and most British bibliographers of note have one time or another held the post. Jenkinson had been appointed lecturer, as I have said, for 1907/8, to deliver six lectures. But 1907 was a black year for him, in which no extra work could be undertaken.

On October 28 he wrote to Duff in a letter which has already been quoted in another connexion (*vide supra*, p. 32):

We have had a sad autumn. At the end of August my brother was taken ill, and after a month of increasing drowsiness, he died on Sept. 27. It proved to be an abscess in the brain for which nothing could have been done. The cause is unknown. It has cut short a very useful and happy life.

Beneath these laconic sentences lay a deep emotion. Jenkinson's love for his brother Charlie, four and a half years his junior, was a very beautiful thing. The two men were in many respects the complement of each other. After a visit to Cambridge, in 1878, Jenkinson writes to his sister, "Yes, Charlie and I both enjoyed his stay here: I think we could live together very well. I was glad to introduce him to some of my friends. Alfred [? A. C. Cole] confided to me the first night that 'he was a sort

[1] Cf. Annual Report of the Library Syndicate for 1894.

of fellow that made you look at your boots.' They all liked him."
Their lives had run in very different channels, but the brothers
when they met found themselves in perfect harmony of taste.
The student followed the fortunes of the soldier in Asia, in
West and South Africa and when he settled down to a country
life in Northamptonshire, with eager excitement and admiration
for his resourcefulness and intelligence. Francis took a very
sane view of man's inevitable end, and never let grief master
him; but there is no doubt that this loss seriously impaired his
power of resistance.

So it was natural that he should put off the performance of
what he regarded at best as an unpleasant duty to the latest
possible date and reduce it to the smallest possible compass,
delivering one single lecture on December 4, 1908.

His topic was one on which he had a right to be heard—the
chronological succession of certain books printed at Cologne by
Ulric Zell between 1466 and 1472, *i.e.* twenty-seven quartos,
the variations in the type and press-work of which he subjected
to a minute, nay microscopic, investigation. The occurrence
of b and þ, of the compound letters ƀ, þo, iŋ, is scrupulously
noted, and the change from four pin-holes to two, and the
reasons therefor. The result is a table of succession which no
one is likely to dispute, leading off, not with the *De Officiis*,
to which Jenkinson would have been glad to give precedence,
as Proctor did, hailing it as possibly the first classical book ever
printed, of which moreover he himself possessed a fine copy, but
with the Chrysostom *Super Psalmum L*, "of which unfortunately
there is no copy in Cambridge."

All this made up what was certainly a highly technica
exposition, but like Bradshaw, the lecturer succeeded in getting
at the man behind the book, and in bringing the compositor
alive and at work before one's eyes, with his experiments upon
page and form of letter, his personal tastes and preferences, his
slips and blunders and attempts at recovery.

Yet though the imagination had free play, there were no
wild and unjustifiable conjectures *à la* P. Madden, "the acute

but perverse," or *à la* Dr Voullième ("to whom," said Jenkinson, "following Proctor, I endeavour to be grateful for what he has done in his list of Cologne fifteenth-century books").

Every statement is proved by detailed illustration, or if not provable but only probable, duly qualified and conditioned. Bradshaw's method—the rigorous marshalling of facts, the use of a provisional hypothesis upon occasion for the sake of grouping facts already ascertained, and of preparing for the next step— this was the only one (all else was mere trifling) which Jenkinson recognized, and of it this paper of twenty-seven pages is a notable example[1].

He did not himself regard it as final—he never "deposited" it in the Library and so never was paid his fee; but that was due to his extreme fastidiousness which now there is, alas! no reason to indulge; and I hope that, thanks to Mr A. W. Pollard and the Bibliographical Society, the slender list of his published works may before long be increased by an important and interesting item.

I quote here as eminently characteristic the last page of his lecture and a couple of relevant entries in his Diary:

And this is all I have time to say about Ulric Zell today. It is a curious thing that although his name has always been a name to conjure with and collectors have felt bound to have specimens of his work, the study of him has never got beyond what I may call the Dibdinesque stage. The books of other printers have been fathered on him, notably those of Conrad Winters, but also many of other Cologne printers; also books printed at Deventer, Geneva, and Rome (in roman character). On the other hand, no attempt has been made to distinguish between the best of his own work, which as we have seen is very good, and the worst, which is extremely bad. Perhaps it is this state of things which has enabled us to accumulate in the University Library the very respectable collection which now stands on the shelves. Certainly the diffusion of knowledge has its drawbacks; and the acquisition of the twenty or so that we still need seems not likely to be accomplished in our time. Of Zell's folios and of his later books in general our series is not very large; and I know too little about them to make any pretence of discussing them.

[1] We find him working at ꝑ, etc., in Chrysostom's *De reparatione lapsi* (Zell) as early as 1891.

Dec. 3rd, 1908. Two letters from G. Dunn, about Zells, of which, as I expected, he knows almost all that I am going to say.

Dec. 4th. Weather most wretched: yet the Master of Peterhouse was there. Jessie's lantern slides were most effective[1]; and nine books in a glass table-case illustrated other points.

His self-comment in a letter to Duff was brief: "My Zell paper came out very clean and nice, unexpectedly so, and pleased me. But of course it is only one small point in a multitude."

He marked the occasion by presenting to the Library his collection of *incunabula*, ninety separate works, and among them the rare *De Officiis* which he had felt himself obliged to place second on his list of Zells.

The year 1911 was signalized by the battle over the Copyright Bill.

The University Library, together with the Bodleian, the Advocates' Library at Edinburgh, and Trinity College, Dublin, has since the reign of Queen Anne possessed the right to claim a copy of every book published in the United Kingdom, a right which is generally and properly regarded as carrying the obligation to preserve the national literature as it grows. The right of the British Museum to have delivered to it upon publication every book, bound and on the best paper, has never been contested. If it were, the story of the first edition of the *Pilgrim's Progress* would have point[2]. But, as we shall presently hear Jenkinson arguing, a solitary copy of a work shut up in the metropolis, although better than nothing, is not enough.

Now, in 1910, there arose a risk that this national duty would be rendered difficult of discharge by the terms of a new Copyright Bill under which the time for claiming books from the publishers was to be reduced from twelve months to three months from the date of publication, which date was not defined. This obviously

[1] Twenty photographs of illustrative pages were taken and turned into slides, fourteen of which were used at the lecture.

[2] Until the latter half of the nineteenth century it was believed that no single copy of the first edition of *The Pilgrim's Progress* was in existence. Then a copy was discovered in a private library. If the work on publication had been deposited in public collections, copies would have been available for general use. What happened to Bunyan would happen to other authors.

would increase the chance of missing books and of impairing the representative character of the University collection. Jenkinson got wind of the proposal and warned the Syndicate at their meeting on October 19 of what was brewing. A Memorandum which is a model of cogent reasoning was drafted by the Provost of King's and himself, and the Syndicate suggested that he should consult the Members of Parliament for the Universities. This he did on two visits to London. On the second occasion, April 6, 1911, when the Bill was on for second reading, he spent a busy but agreeable day at the House of Commons, seeing old friends and making new acquaintances (*e.g.* John Burns: "He wants the passage from Gildas about the *instabilitas* of the Welsh, about whom he surmises we think alike") and exploring the building: "Finally they took me along the beautiful passages with groined roofs, and shewed me the room where Charles I's death-warrant was signed."

The Bill was read a second time on April 7, when "Sir William Anson, as I saw in the *Times* next morning, said all that had to be said: and Larmor and Rawlinson accordingly refrained from speaking." But in Committee six weeks later Mr Rawlinson carried an amendment restoring the threatened twelve months, and also securing the very valuable condition whereby a claim for the first part of a periodical publication involved a claim for the whole. The situation was thus safe in the Lower House. But there remained the Lords, to whom the Bill was sent up in the autumn.

The Publishers' Association, alarmed and exasperated by the addition of the National Library of Wales to the number of privileged libraries (an obvious sop to the Welsh supporters of the Government), issued a manifesto, an appeal *ad misericordiam*, imploring the House of Lords to "exercise its beneficent legislative influence and deliver them from the gross and singular injustice of having to supply five copies of every book gratis. They prayed that clause 15 should be so amended that not only no further burden may be put upon them but if possible some guarantee may be given that the intention of the Act [of 1842] will be carried out in the spirit in which the grant of free copies was originally made to academic bodies, viz. that they shall require...none but such books as can be of value in academic libraries." It will be observed that no reference was made to the patriotic obligation to preserve the national literature upon which the University Libraries took their stand. Jenkinson describes the effect of this manifesto upon the Library authorities:

Monday, November 13. At Book Recommendation Sub-syndicate a telegram from Shipley[1] at Manchester, calling attention to publishers' memorandum to House of Lords which is in committee on Copyright Bill tomorrow. So to Library, then drove off for Aldis, called on Jackson, Larmor (away), V. C. (engaged tonight), Gaselee (out), Provost...and so home at 8.10. After dinner wrote to Hallam Tennyson and to Rawlinson.

Shipley's telegram contained the spirited suggestion that all Oxford and Cambridge peers and bishops should be whipped up at once. This explains the next entry:

November 14. Just after dinner a telegram from Rawlinson. Went off to Christ's and found Shipley, who set to work, Marshall helping, and another. By 10.15 we had sent nearly 50 telegrams to Cambridge peers. Starry night.

The eloquence of the publishers touched the hearts of a number of noble lords, and on November 15 Lord Gorell moved an amendment to the effect that the choice of books supplied by them to the libraries should be controlled, and suggested as the controlling body—the Board of Trade! Lord Cromer supported him in a speech which shewed something less than intelligence of the position. He enlarged upon the un-suitability of certain books for dons or undergraduates, *e.g. The Story of Emma, Lady Hamilton*, profusely illustrated. Lord Curzon of Kedleston had no difficulty in demolishing so flimsy a structure and in defending the Bodleian as something more than a mere academic institution grinding grist for tutors and their pupils. He was followed on the same side by

[1] Sir Arthur Shipley, Master of Christ's.

Lord Courtney of Penwith, speaking for Cambridge, Lord Ashbourne for Ireland, and the Archbishop of Canterbury, sprinkling humour and common sense on the debate. The amendment was lost and Mr Rawlinson telegraphed at night "Clause saved by 29 to 15: heartiest congratulations."

But it was plain that the publishers were not willing to accept defeat. Accordingly the University on November 18 put out a reply to them in which the hand of Jenkinson is plainly visible; all in fact, except the concluding paragraph, is his:

Nov. 18. A letter from John Murray in the *Times*: and other indications that the attack will be renewed in the Report stage. Shipley came in, and recommended an immediate memorandum to the Lords. So, after writing to Hallam Tennyson (who did not get my letter in time!), Rawlinson, etc., I drafted something while I ate my sandwiches. 2.30 the V.-C., Shipley, and McLean came in, amended and added a last paragraph, and I took the copy to press at 3.0. I went and had a talk with the Ma^r of Peterhouse. Then just got in my letters...with extra $\frac{1}{2}d$.'s rather by special favour, I think. Then had some tea sent in from Trinity for those who were working. 4.45 saw a proof, and passed it. 6.0 750 copies came from the Press, and by 7.0 all were posted. Also I sent copies to Rawlinson, Anson, Dickson, H. A. Wilson. Left some for the Ma^r of Peterhouse and got home at 7.30.

Here is the Cambridge Memorandum:

I. The Publishers in their memorandum ignore the national importance of preserving a record of the national literature. This must be done automatically, or it will not be done at all. The one copy sent to the British Museum is not sufficient; it is liable to destruction by wear and tear, not to mention the risks of fire, mutilation, and theft. Moreover it is to the advantage of students that there should be more than one centre at which they can be sure of finding the books they require. The right to claim books has been more and more regarded as a right which in the public interest ought to be exercised. Consequently the collections now contained in the four Libraries are more comprehensive and representative of the literature of the country than they would have been if the selection of books had been governed merely by considerations of immediate practical utility; and the Libraries have come to be in this respect of national importance. Very strong arguments ought to be required before the abolition of these conditions is even contemplated: no such arguments have been brought forward.

II. The inference from history is irrelevant and can hardly be meant seriously. If the deposit of copies was in the seventeenth century connected with the literary censorship, that connexion has so long ceased that it is now not generally remembered. The utility of the present practice from a public point of view is obvious; and a system that is advantageous to students and authors is probably directly or indirectly advantageous also to publishers. The question is whether the burden put upon the trade is so heavy as some of the publishers assert.

In the case of ordinary books the cost of printing five extra copies is so small that it may be neglected. When a book contains illustrations coloured by hand, the libraries pay for the hand colouring. Between these two classes, there are expensive scientific books, illustrated but not coloured by hand. Here if anywhere the cost of printing five extra copies may be perceptible, or might even be considerable if it were not spread over the whole impression. But these expensive scientific books are precisely those which by common consent the Libraries would be *expected* to claim. It is therefore not easy to see what the publishers would gain by the selection being limited, though it is easy to see that the Libraries as centres of general usefulness would suffer.

III. The authorities at Cambridge recognize that the University Library owes much to the existing law, and they welcome the statement of Mr John Murray in the *Times* of 18th November, 1911, that "If the Government had left things as they were, instead of embodying this late Welsh afterthought in the Bill, the publishers would not have raised any protest."

This drew another letter to the *Times* from Mr Murray which Jenkinson answered on November 21 in a tone of gentle banter: "My friend Mr John Murray will forgive me if I suggest that his letter in the *Times* of today is written with less than his accustomed lucidity. *Facit indignatio versum*: indignation is apt to turn things upside down." He proceeded to set the matter in its right posture and vindicate the Memorandum.

There was further correspondence *de part et d'autre* with which we need not concern ourselves.

Meanwhile a peer was found willing to push the publishers' case in the person of Lord Montague of Beaulieu. The first news of his action was conveyed to Cambridge by a telegram from Sir William Anson to Jenkinson on December 4: "Dangerous amendment in the Lords." Jenkinson telegraphed at once to Mr Rawlinson, the Duke of Devonshire and Mr Steel-Maitland (whom he had recently met at Stirling when staying with Mr W. G. Crum). Lord Montague had tabled two amendments to the Bill: (1) "that all demands for books except in the case of the British Museum shall be made in writing direct to the publisher by the librarian, and it shall be understood that no book will be asked for which is not intended to be permanently added to the library for which it is claimed," and (2) that in the event of dispute there should be appeal to an arbitrator appointed by the Treasury, whose judgement should be final. Both amendments were, however, withdrawn under the battery of Lord Ashbourne, Lord Balfour of Burleigh, Lord Rayleigh, and Lord Curzon, and Rawlinson telegraphed that night "amendment lost," and the defenders of the libraries could rest on their laurels.

Upon the whole question of publishers and libraries it may be remarked, leaving aside the higher motives, that the conditions of copyright are incident to a particular calling which is not that of butcher, baker, or candlestick-maker, a calling upon which no one need enter with shut eyes.

I have dwelt at some length on this copyright affair, not from a desire to bathe in stagnant waters, but because I have to vindicate Jenkinson from the imputation which has been airily thrown about that he was casual, slack, and needing to be stirred to action. Certainly he needed to be stirred to action, for he was a lover of peace, but it was by the events themselves or by those whose vigilance foresaw them. Once aroused, his activity was as his strength, and his fire and energy amazed his friends. It is no more true that he was slothful in business than that he was puzzled by library finance.

The controversy was not without its humorous and good-tempered side. On July 15, 1911, Jenkinson writes to his sister:

At a dinner last Saturday I sat next Mr Fisher Unwin who has been protesting in the *Times* against our Copyright privileges! and John Murray was near. We had rather a laugh about it.

After this conflict there came a period of repose before the cataclysm of 1914. The next two years were uneventful for the Library and its chief, save for acquisitions recorded further on and for the inevitable thinning of the ranks of benefactors such as J. E. Foster, J. H. Ellis (who had nobly responded to the Appeal of 1905), and W. G. Searle, whose voice and figure, learning and assiduity are still remembered by many.

Chapter VII

THE WAR COLLECTION

THE War, with its tale of splendour and misery, stirred Jenkinson profoundly. His patriotism was intense and often expressed with surprising vehemence. Irish rebels and pro-Germans of whatever nationality stood in his esteem a degree below the enemy; "pacifists" and "defeatists" were not far off, although he respected conscience and was against compulsion.

He was of course unfit for any form of active service, and he held his post of duty to be the Library, but his serenity and cheerfulness were a valuable asset in days of depression. From the first battle of Le Cateau (how he would have rejoiced at the final vindication of his well-loved cousin Sir Horace Smith-Dorrien!) to the last battle of the Sambre, his confidence in our cause and our arms never faltered; or if it did he did not shew it, for he had a nerve-racked household to reassure. Death barely touched his own immediate family[1] but the loss of his friends' sons—John Tilley, Erasmus Darwin, Ralph Aldis, Jock McEwen, Francis Pemberton, Maurice and Edward Gray, Patrick and Donald McLeod Innes—moved him as if they had been his own. He formed ties with many of the cadets training for commissions in Trinity, especially with such as shared any of his tastes—music, books, insects—and he was eager to interest them in what throughout those four years lay next his heart—his War Collection.

At the beginning of 1915 he foresaw the production of an extensive if ephemeral literature, and he determined to catch it as it grew. He was not content, as were some libraries, to wait until the turmoil was past and then purchase a collection

[1] His young cousin and heir to the baronetcy, John Banks Jenkinson fell in action on September 14, 1914.

ready made. Such a method, slothful, mechanical, unimaginative, was not his. He set to work at once, writing in all directions, literally from China to Peru, to public offices at home and abroad, to men on every front, to English exiles, to sympathetic neutrals. Whenever he saw an announcement or read a letter in the press which indicated a likely source to tap, he established contact. Nothing came amiss to his net; all the straws on the torrent were diligently salved. Here is an example of his direct appeal:

University Library, Cambridge. September 22, 1916.
Dear Sir,

I see in the *Morning Post* reference to the *Fifth Gloucester Gazette*, and your name is mentioned in connexion with the poems of Lieut. F. W. Harvey. I am making great efforts to get together a War Collection for preservation in this Library, as likely to be interesting hereafter and also useful. I have a certain number of trench magazines, etc., but I have *not* this. Can you help me to get a set? Or pass this on to some one who can and will? So many of these publications will disappear after the War that copies ought to be housed in a few safe places.

Believe me,
Yours faithfully,
FRANCIS JENKINSON,
Librarian.
Colonel J. H. COLLETT, C.M.G.

He procured the insertion of a Spanish paragraph asking for help in the *America Latina*, a monthly journal published in London, and he gladly sanctioned the like use of the *Cambridge Magazine*—an organ with which he had scant sympathy—because it had special facilities for procuring what he wanted. He spent hours entering donations and stamping them with his own hand, and pending a final and comprehensive acknowledgement he recorded gifts and progress in successive Reports of the Syndicate.

Thus in May, 1915, he writes:

An attempt is being made to form a historical collection of pamphlets, newspapers, proclamations, fly-sheets, etc., illustrative of the War. Some of the most desirable things are perhaps impossible to obtain; but it is hoped that Members of the University and other friends who have special opportunities will be able and willing to help. Something has been done in this way already.

The same theme is repeated with variations in 1916, and *diminuendo* till the end, with occasional "lifts" such as a set of the *Bulletin des Armées* from Lord Esher in 1917 and a series of French coloured posters from Mr W. Crum Watson in 1920:

A special effort has been made to collect, while it is still possible, such ephemeral literature arising out of the War as might hereafter be interesting and useful to students. German propaganda literature has been accumulated chiefly from Italy, Spain, the United States, and some of the South American Republics. Much of this is printed in Germany; but some is produced by partizans at Genoa, Barcelona, Castellon, New York, Chicago, Shanghai, Bogotá, Medellin, Barranquilla, San José, Santiago, Curaçoa, etc. All serial publications, newspapers, pamphlets, posters, leaflets, etc., connected with the War have been welcomed, and much help has been given by kind friends, both here and abroad. (These gifts are entered in a special donation book; and it is hoped that in due time a full account will be issued, together with the names of the donors. At present the Syndicate think it advisable to content themselves with this general acknowledgement. In the meantime they appeal to Members of the University and other friends to do what they can to make the collection cover as much ground as possible.)

The mass of material grew ultimately too big for his hands (though he continued writing up the list of donations till March, 1920) and the staff stepped in and relieved him of the burden, though not of the general oversight[1].

No one grumbled, because he had infected them all with his enthusiasm, but it may be they grudged the heavy demand made upon their diminished strength. It was sometimes hinted, though not inside the Library, that the Librarian's energies would have been better employed in completing his work on the fifteenth-century books which he alone could do and which

[1] For the final classification of the collection as achieved in 1921, see Appendix.

was never done. And possibly had he foreseen how short his time was he might have paused. But there can be no doubt that he rendered a public service, and that some day the historian or psychologist will turn with avidity to the ill-printed scraps, often stained with the Flanders mud, to the pages of *The Grim Old Lion's Dare Devil's Gazette* or *The Two-Asuere*, and bless the man who managed to save them from the dust heap. In any case, for the purpose of this memoir which is, however feebly, to depict a character, the fact that a man aged sixty-two, of small health, whose real interest lay in art and entomology and Low Country quartos, who ten years before had openly complained that the Acton Library held so few of these—that he should for the sake of posterity have taken this plunge into history in the making, is valuable as evidence of mental alertness, vision, and initiatory genius[1].

Just before War broke out a movement, fraught with happy results, was set on foot mainly by Aldis and A. G. W. Murray to commemorate the Librarian's twenty-five years of service to learning and to the University by a portrait which should hang in the Library. Through the good offices of Sir Charles Walston, John Sargent, though he was supposed to have given up portrait-painting, was induced to undertake the commission, and on January 28, 1915, the sittings, or rather the standings, began. Jenkinson had looked forward to them with apprehension, but sympathy between the two men was at once established, and what was on both sides undoubtedly a labour proved also a delight.

On the one hand Jenkinson declared that "the painful penalties of standing still for two hours at a time were more than he had thought possible," while no one who ever saw the great artist at his work is likely to forget the mental and physical energy of the effort—the deep breaths, the feverish mixing of colours on the palette, the rushes to and fro between the artist's

[1] If this record should chance to meet the eye of Señor Francisco Carbonell of Barcelona or of Mr Charles Stewart Davison of New York, they will be glad to be reminded of the pleasure they gave to a man who was worth pleasing by their ready and generous response to his appeal.

stance and the canvas, placed close up against the model, the swift touches under which the dull black surface shimmered into silk.

But tired nature demanded pauses, and then he would switch on to his gramophone a Fauré record or a Spanish folk-song and smoke a cigarette while Jenkinson stood at ease offering comments—on the Fauré, "Very reminiscent of Brahms"—on the folk-song, "That stuff is at the bottom of all good music." And so to work again, till at last on March 20 Jenkinson notes: "Said good-bye to Sargent, regretfully," and the picture was left alone with its maker. He was without doubt pleased with it and with his subject, and said so to more than one hearer. His satisfaction is apparent in the work: "Sargent evidently liked you better than he did Curzon," wrote George Prothero on seeing the two portraits by the same hand in the Academy. And there is no doubt that the Jenkinson portrait is really one of Sargent's successes. It is at once dignified and pleasant. Qualities which he did not always display in equal proportion are here in almost perfect balance; the amazing technical dexterity interprets character without obscuring it. Certainly it is a worthy memorial. Yet it is not the whole man. The sweetness and the grace are there, but not the fire of his unquenched youth, nor on the other hand the lines and wrinkles which age had drawn upon the beautiful face. When Sargent's attention was directed to their absence he refused to add them and "make a railway system of him."

Having served its turn at Burlington House the picture was ceremoniously offered to the University on December 7 in the Combination Room at Trinity, not without speech-making by the Masters of Trinity, Emmanuel, and Peterhouse, Sir Charles Walston, the Provost of King's, who made the presentation, and the President of Queens', who as Vice-Chancellor received it.

Dr James struck the right note, and his words are so true a summary of Jenkinson's librarianship that they must be quoted if only in the *oratio obliqua* of the *Cambridge Daily News*:

The Provost of King's said they were met together upon a very pleasant occasion. They did not often have a chance of expressing in a public and formal manner the thanks to those who, living among them for many years, had done, and were still doing, work of the first importance to the University. But when such an occasion did come round, and when coupled with it there was the opportunity of enriching the University itself with a possession of high value—although representing the givers, he must say that—then the occasion was doubly satisfactory. The part which the Library played in University life was highly important, and at the same time deeply unobtrusive, and to maintain it full and clear and free from confusion they had need of many ministers of different qualifications, some to acquire and get more, some to arrange and order and distribute, and at the head of them they wanted one man who should be alive to all the great and small activities of the whole organism, the main lines of policy and the tiny details of administration, and to the manifold interests and great traditions of that reservoir of knowledge which had supplied Cambridge for the past 500 years. Such a man they had in Mr Jenkinson. (Applause.) For over a quarter of a century he had been in the position. So dear a friend and close a follower of Henry Bradshaw could not have been otherwise. To the world outside he had stood forth as a Librarian instantly and continuously ready to help. There was no place where scholars, either within or without, could find a more kindly and appreciative reception. There was nothing in Mr Jenkinson's librarianship that he (the speaker) contemplated with greater pleasure than the atmosphere of friendliness which had surrounded that band of workers and had animated every one. It had been a spirit fostered by their chief and by the ideals they had seen that he followed. (Applause.) One thing that he (the speaker) found specially important was the extraordinary range of Mr Jenkinson's interest. Nothing was too great or too small for him. They could see that his interest in the small things was due to the fact that it was only possible because he saw them as a part of a greater whole, and no one who knew him would ever attempt to suggest that he was not susceptible to the things that were really great in art and life. After alluding to the list of University Librarians, and remarking that the last four names on the list (J. E. B. Mayor, H. Bradshaw, W. Robertson Smith and F. Jenkinson) were names that everyone in that room instinctively regarded with reverence and affection—

(applause)—the Provost said that when he put it to them that in that picture the greatest painter of his time had perpetuated a beloved personality, he might be excused if he dwelt upon the value of what he had to offer. Turning to the Vice-Chancellor, the Provost concluded: "On behalf of the subscribers I beg to offer it, through you, to the University."

Later in the proceedings the pressman, yielding to a sound instinct, resumes direct speech for a moment in reporting Dr Adolphus Ward:

"We are all proud of our Library; there are all kinds of books, but there is no work in the Library which can compete in interest with the Librarian." He was loved by all, loved by his staff, loved by his visitors, and loved by his books, he had sometimes thought, when he had observed how Mr Jenkinson manipulated them when they came into his hands.

Jenkinson, who found "the whole thing very pleasant, free from stiffness," in reply to all this eulogy avoided as far as he possibly could all mention of himself. He sketched the aspect of the Library as it was in 1889 and at that moment. He welcomed the presence of many colleagues, especially Mr H. T. Francis, recently retired, and Mr Aldis, the Librarian's Secretary, for whom, as for his office, Cambridge was indebted to the energy and judgement of the late Mr J. W. Clark[1].

Finally, speaking of his association with Mr Bradshaw, the speaker remarked that he had only worked at books with him during the last three years of his life, but he absorbed some of his ideas and tried to carry them out as far as he could. It was a pity some other of those ideas had not been taken up by more competent people, but he hoped they would be carried out some day. In conclusion, Mr Jenkinson gracefully testified to the feelings of reverence and respect entertained by the whole of the staff for Mr Bradshaw.

It was like him to divert the stream of praise from himself on to the memory of his beloved Master.

[1] Died 1910.

Chapter VIII

LIBRARY EXTENSION

FROM 1918 to 1921 various schemes for the extension of the Library were launched and wrecked. First came the return, in a greatly modified form, to the old device of roofing in the Eastern Quadrangle to provide a Reading Room, somewhat after the manner of the Marciana Library (which strangely enough does not appear to have been referred to publicly in this connexion). The book-stores this time were to be sunk in the ground below the two quadrangles[1]. But this plan was abandoned as soon as the architect presented his estimate, for, as the Syndicate sagaciously observed, a subterranean chamber would not touch the heart of the great public, to whom appeal must be made for the large sum required for excavation. This objection held equally of the suggestion of a vast store such as they have at Oxford, contrived under the lawn of Senate House yard. It did not, however, apply to the next proposal of a building on the south side of the yard, parallel to the Senate House, and similar in appearance, thus completing Gibbs's original plan[2]. Opposition was at once offered on aesthetic grounds—"It would dwarf King's Chapel" (an obviously futile argument); "It would obscure the view of the Senate House." This was a serious consideration, and one which Jenkinson himself must have felt. Many years before, in 1905, I find in his Diary:

March 26, W. Sunny. Trumpington Street, as I walked in with Sayle, was looking its very best; especially where the Gate of Honour is visible straight ahead, flanked by the King's and Library group on the left, Corpus forming the frame on the right, all brilliantly clear, even to some red blinds in the small court of Caius.

It was evident from the Discussion on March 4, 1920, that the proposal could not succeed.

Two alternatives then remained. Either form a *dépendance* or dump somewhere to which books not likely to be wanted

---

[1] Cf. *Reporter* for 1918/19, pp. 675, 789 ff.
[2] Cf. *Reporter* for 1919/20, pp. 657 ff.

should be removed (as the British Museum has done with its periodicals) or go boldly for a brand new Library on a new site. Jenkinson, who had kept very quiet all through the debates, had come to see that this was the only way out of the *impasse* and as member of the Syndicate which recommended it he signed on February 9, 1921, without faltering the death-warrant of the Library as he had known it all his Cambridge life.

Of course he shared the feelings of the minority who protested against the desertion of the ancient site, but he was aware that it must come, although he did not expect to see it accomplished. The new proposal once adopted and blessed by Professor Ridgeway and other veteran opponents of the Eastern Quadrangle scheme, it only remained to find a site[1]. This was at first to be the Corpus cricket ground, near Selwyn, but soon a more convenient place was found on the Clare and King's field which, still covered with the relics of the First Eastern General Hospital, now awaits its final destiny[2].

Jenkinson was not by nature a good beggar; but although he did not often screw himself up to ask, he always earnestly desired; and the naïve, child-like delight with which he accepted gifts for his beloved library rendered it a pleasure to bestow them and no doubt stimulated the stream. Within three months of his election I find him writing to Mr Christopher Wordsworth: "I wish you could wake up somebody to give or leave us something. Our benefactors are a very scanty body: and no one can say we don't take care of things now."

The foregoing sketch of his stewardship contains already several instances of the fulfilment of this aspiration—the Sandars bequests, the Acton Library, the response to the appeal of 1905— and now, by way of *envoi* I here record certain other benefactions which especially gladdened his heart during those thirty-four years. There were Professor Couch Adams's early printed books in 1892; books from Clare Lodge in 1915 (I cite without reference to chronological order); the J. W. Clark Cambridge

[1] Cf. *Reporter* for 1920/21, pp. 732 ff. [2] Cf. *Reporter* for 1921/22, pp. 978 ff.

84

collection; modern MSS.—Shelley (from Col. Call, the son-in-law of Trevelyan), Tennyson (from his old friend the second Lord)—gifts in kind and in money from Ingram Bywater, J. E. B. Mayor, W. Aldis Wright, J. H. Ellis, George Dunn, E. G. Duff, A. G. W. Murray, C. Sayle, not to mention many living donors whose names are in the *Annual Reports* and who will be glad to remember the welcome with which their generosity was received.

Notable additions were constantly being made to the Oriental department, ancient and modern, associated with the names of Robertson Smith, R. L. Bensly, F. Chance, Sir T. Wade, R. J. Wilkinson, E. B. Cowell.

Above all there was the transference in bulk to Cambridge of the Cairo "Genizah," 40,000 fragments of Jewish "superseded" literature, procured by the devotion of Dr Solomon Schechter and made ours by the munificence of Dr C. Taylor[1]. From that pestiferous wrack[2], among much else of interest the Rabbi recovered fragments of the Hebrew *Ecclesiasticus*, and Professor Burkitt, to Jenkinson's great delight, a sixth-century palimpsest of a bit of Aquila[2].

Other Oriental *aubaines* of romantic interest were a volume of the great Chinese Encyclopedia, literally plucked from the burning of Han-lin College at Peking and presented by Mr Lancelot Giles in 1901 and other wrack of the same storm, viz. nine gold-engraved jade tablets picked up by Frank Norris, one of Jenkinson's favourite pupils at Trinity, now Bishop of North China. But the acquisition which perhaps excited Jenkinson most of all during his librarianship was that of the Utrecht *Doctrinale* (a rhymed Latin Grammar), in 1913.

There is a group of early Low Country books known as "Costeriana" from the name of one L. J. Coster their supposed

---

1 The late Master of St John's marked each decade by some princely gift. In 1889 it was his year's stipend as Vice-Chancellor; in 1897 the Genizah; in 1907 the Kanjur, the great Tibetan translation of northern Buddhist canonical books, which had long been desired by students of Buddhist Sanskrit (*v.s.* p. 62). This was put in order by Miss C. M. Ridding.

2 Dr Schechter seriously damaged his health by his labours. No one who saw him in his nose-bag among the débris is likely to forget it.

3 Cf. the *Times* of August 3, 1897—letters by Dr Schechter and F. C. Burkitt.

printer at Haarlem[1]. These have always been a mystery. Fragments had been recovered from bindings, etc., of some fifty—editions of the *Doctrinale* of Donatus, and so on—but there was, and is, only one complete book of the class known to exist, and very few knew of it. This is a small 4° of ninety-two pages which had once belonged (an added interest) to an English merchant of the staple, living at Calais. The precious volume turned up, among "other properties," in a London sale on August 4, 1896. The catalogue description though vague and brief was enough to draw from Jenkinson a telegram and a commission. The bookseller made a muddle and let the book slip. It was knocked down to Mr George Dunn of Woolley Park for £23. Jenkinson's disappointment—"So much for commissions"—was mitigated or enhanced by the discovery that the volume was what he had guessed it to be, an unknown Costerianum, complete, and hence of first-rate importance in the history of Low Country printing. Mr R. Proctor wrote from the British Museum to condole and congratulate. "I fully sympathize with your ill-fortune, but you have at least the consolation of having spotted it. To our disgrace we knew nothing about it."

Now Mr Dunn, though not acquainted with Jenkinson at the time, came to be a good friend to the University Library and had often expressed his intention of leaving *incunabula* to it, including the *Doctrinale*. He, however, died in 1912, intestate, and so his books came to the hammer. The auctioneers were apparently as ignorant as ever of the real value of this item, and most London booksellers were equally unenlightened. Not so the British Museum, who, however, would not have bidden against Cambridge; nor the Dutch bibliographers, more formidable rivals, who were prepared to go beyond any figure that we could compass, despite the obvious duty of increasing, if possible, the incomparable collection begun by Bradshaw. Jenkinson was despondent. "If Dunn had lived," he wrote, "it

[1] Cf. E. Gordon Duff, *Early Printed Books* (1893), pp. 95 ff.

would probably have come here eventually. It is doubly sad to lose him *and* his books *and* so much of his work."

At this point in stepped Mr John Charrington of Trinity, whose interest and generosity were kindled by A. G. W. Murray, also of Trinity, a young man of singular bibliographical flair, who afterwards, largely by Jenkinson's recommendation, became Librarian to his College. Mr Charrington determined to secure the *Doctrinale* for the University Library. Jenkinson was immensely touched and pleased and excited—"much too excited to sleep." To Murray he wrote, "I thought that no one cared a button about U.L.C. *incunabula*....It ought to give one a fresh start to find that there is a present as well as a past." To Mr Charrington he said, "Whether you succeed or not, it is a great encouragement to find such enthusiasm aroused in behalf of a not very popular cause; and I shall never forget it."

The coveted object came up for sale on February 13. The bidding was keen. The minion of the Dutch forced the price up far above what Dunn had given for it in 1896; but Mr Charrington was not to be denied. Despite the ominous date, Friday, February 13, 1913, he emerged triumphant from the contest, and Jenkinson carried off the *Doctrinale* there and then.

It was almost to a day the 260th anniversary of Van Tromp's defeat by Blake, as Mr Charrington was careful to record on the picture (Sir Joshua's Duke of Gloucester) with which he presented the Librarian in honour of the day.

Let it be added, to round off the story, that the Library Syndicate voted £100 towards the cost of the *Doctrinale* and that Jenkinson, wanting, as he said, " to have a finger in the pie," sent Mr Charrington a valuable book of his own either to keep or to sell and count the value as so much off the price he had paid in the sale-room. But the donor preferred to take the whole expense upon himself.

Jenkinson told the first part of the story, how he had missed the *Doctrinale* in 1896, to the assembled librarians at their meeting in 1905; such a happy conclusion was beyond his wildest hopes.

Chapter IX

BIBLIOGRAPHICAL AND
LITERARY STUDIES

SO far we have seen Jenkinson in the Library, helping others and occupied with administration. There was scant time in his crowded day for what is called in Cambridge "your own work," work which is not only an obligation but a happiness[1], even for those bibliographical and antiquarian pursuits for which the place supplied opportunity and in which he excelled. Of his mastery in the matter of Low Country printing, freely acknowledged by many disciples, the only visible monuments are the Sandars lecture above mentioned[2] and the *List of the Incunabula collected by George Dunn* which Mr A. W. Pollard carried off in manuscript on Jenkinson's last day in Cambridge and published posthumously as a supplement to the *Transactions of the Bibliographical Society.* This is a catalogue of the Woolley Hall fifteenth-century books (as sold at Sotheby's in four instalments, realizing £32,390. 15s. 6d. between February, 1913, and November, 1917) arranged according to country, town, and printer, *i.e.* in Proctor's order, which was Bradshaw's, which was Jenkinson's. It is a worthy memorial of the three men.

Mention must also be made of a delicious note on a volume from the Library of the Dominicans of Dundee, written in 1902 for the Edinburgh Bibliographical Society and issued in their *Proceedings* of 1906. The book in question contains three pieces printed at Utrecht and Louvain in 1474 and 1475 (?)

[1] I remember his saying, when a friend went into hospital determined to resist the order to read nothing but trash: "Doctors don't always understand that work which is a pleasure does no harm."

[2] It is hoped that this may ere long see the light of print (*vide supra*, p. 68), as also the systematic catalogue of incunables in the University Library which was left unfinished—*Pendent opera interrupta.*

which had been bought in the latter year by one Henry Barry, rector of Collace in the Carse of Gowrie, and which passed through many hands, some of which are recorded on its blank leaves, until it came to rest with Bradshaw in 1879. Jenkinson described it in general terms and posed to the members of the Society a number of pertinent questions. Who was Henry Barry? What is known of the Black Friars to whom he gave the book? Who were the Ogilvies, father and son, who possessed it later?

Of all these things I am entirely ignorant; and my only excuse for writing this note is that I am fond of the book, which has been for twelve years in my custody, and that I hope to draw some information concerning it from Scottish antiquaries and genealogists.... The Society is indebted to Mr Aldis for much trouble spent in procuring the photographs which illustrate my description of the book. And I am inclined to think that but for his excellence in the maieutic art this paper, such as it is, would never have seen the light.

His wish was gratified by Mr A. H. Millar who in a learned article in *The Dundee Advertiser* of December 20, 1906, identified most of the persons whose names were scribbled in the volume.

To the London Bibliographical Society (of which he was president for the years 1901–1902) he rendered a great service by editing for them in 1896 a paper by M. Claudin on the first Paris Press, though he did not suffer his name to appear when the essay was issued by them as one of their Illustrated Monographs in 1898.

In his presidential address on taking office he aired his grievance against the bookbinders who slit the bottom of pages; in that on taking leave he procured a letter of congratulation to the venerable Léopold Delisle on his jubilee as a librarian, and said a special word in praise of Bernard Quaritch and his cataloguer Mr M. Kerney, "whose genuine enthusiasm makes it a pleasure to go into the auction room at Sotheby's and find him there." Finally, reviewing the ten years of the Society's existence he mentioned as notable occurrences the foundation of the Sandars lectureship, the revival of the Palaeographical Society, the great improvement in booksellers' catalogues and the unfortunate craze for collecting book plates.

Apart from what I have mentioned he did little visible work for any of the bodies whose object it is to further bibliography, partly from lack of health and leisure, partly from an excessive sensitiveness and a fear lest he should be led away from the strait path of the Bradshaw tradition. This I think explains his attitude towards the Henry Bradshaw Society, which deserves a passage to itself.

One of Henry Bradshaw's latest desires was an Ordinal Series, *i.e.* a collection of texts illustrating the growth of the Sarum Ordinal from Richard and Clement Maydeston onwards "with something introductory to shew the real pedigree of the whole thing. I am sure it could be done very satisfactorily," he wrote to Mr Christopher Wordsworth in June, 1882[1], "but some research has yet to be made, before knowledge sufficient for such a book can be gained. This with a *Legenda + Collectarius* would form an invaluable series, a beginning of an English liturgical series."

This aspiration seemed in a fair way of fulfilment when in the summer of 1890 a group of ecclesiastical antiquaries projected a club for the printing of rare liturgical texts which it was first intended to call by the name of Clement Maydeston but which was finally launched in the autumn of that year under that of Henry Bradshaw, in gratitude for his memory and work. Jenkinson was elected a Vice-President and remained so to the end. He went up to the inaugural meeting about which he notes: "Nov. 25, 1890. First meeting of the H.B. Society in the Jerusalem Chamber. Lord Beauchamp in the chair. Then Council meeting at Micklethwaite's till 7. Some anti-Catholic sectarian feeling about. Protested." This was not a happy beginning.

He had not the sympathy with the Society which his loyalty to the man whose name it bore would lead one to expect. Some light upon this apparent anomaly is thrown by the objection raised

[1] Cf. The Cambridge ed. of the *Sarum Breviary*, fasc. iii, p. lxv.

by some Oxonians that the name Bradshaw might suggest connexion with railway time-tables. Minds however learned and pious in which such a notion could lodge for a moment even jocosely were leagues apart from his. But, as I have already said, he was not interested, like Bradshaw, in liturgies for their own sake, and he was rather shy of anything savouring of partizanship in the Church—he shuddered when the term "Anglican" was applied to Dr Hort. In fact he never felt quite at home with the Society. Writing to Mr Christopher Wordsworth, his good friend and Bradshaw's, in November, 1914, he says: "I did not realize that the H.B. Council met at Oxford[1]. It must have been very pleasant. I wish I could have been there. But I am no use for the objects of the Society." Here he was mistaken. Although he was seldom able to attend London meetings, his advice as to the choice of books to edit, and on practical details of typography, was greatly valued, and his replies to inquiry by letter bore fruit. For instance, in the matter of stops, he held strong opinions, inherited from Bradshaw, "against clumsy expedients (such as ꝫ or ·∙) for partially reproducing features of old writing or printing. If they are important," he said, "there ought to be types cut that would look as if they belonged to the fount, which these odd types never do. The type-cutter should *see* the fount his type is to match and should be *made* to match it."

In later issues of the Society's books the disfigurements of which he complained are absent, which seems to shew that his views were adopted.

Again on one occasion about thirty years ago Mr Wordsworth remembers someone, who was very anxious to have a rare book reproduced at all costs, suggesting that it might be put under glass and turned over page by page as the compositor set up the type. Jenkinson said, "I know the book, but I don't see how any ordinary compositor could set up from it. Do you realize that they are men at about 15s. a week and that they have not learned to read such stuff?" He then went on to explain how the thing

---

[1] During the War when train service was disorganized, the President and Fellows of Magdalen invited the Council to meet in their Common Room.

might be done under his own eye in the University Library in a businesslike way, and offered his personal help to supervise the work.

Once he had been reading a preface which displeased him. His remark was, "I might not know much about the subject; but there are many points in which I could make this preface a little more *classical*. The want of arrangement is what really bothers me. However it is no good crying over spilt milk. If I can help in the next book, I will gladly do so."

As long as the Society was run on lines laid down by Bradshaw it had his blessing, but any divergence from these made him cry out.

It is delightful to have Ricemarch's *Martyrology*[1] actually in print. But how could Lawlor make Bradshaw say the original form was *Rhygyvarch*? Do correct it in your copy. We shall have some fool saying what an ignorant man Henry Bradshaw must have been. It is enough to bring H. B. up out of his grave.

Jenkinson's genuine interest in service books as *monumenta* appears from other letters to Mr Wordsworth written in May, 1887, two years before his appointment as Librarian, while he was a free-lance.

I wish some of you church people could stimulate the formation of a fund for buying service books. They become more unprocurable every year, and we really ought to have more, especially as the Bodleian people do nothing to keep unique books in the country[2]. I do not see how I can help much; although I am willing to go up and examine books, and in general to do the executive part. I feel without money it is no use. And there must be people who *would* help. At present, except Mr Sandars no one *does* that I know of.... The Librarian[3] is quite in favour of such a fund as I suggested; but it is not easy to make a move *here*, because people always think in the back of their minds that we residents are specially interested; they cannot understand a disinterested enthusiasm for making ours a main centre of reference in an important subject, and turning

[1] *The Psalter and Martyrology of Ricemarch*, edited by Dr H. J. Lawlor, 2 vols., 1914.

[2] This apparently refers to a Sarum Antiphoner which the Oxford authorities allowed to slip through their fingers.

[3] W. Robertson Smith.

to account books that otherwise remain (or become) isolated and therefore unavailable curiosities.

Account must next be given of an independent achievement in which Jenkinson's knowledge of palaeography and his classical scholarship were put to the test with singular success.

Perhaps the strangest monument of civilized language in the world is the *Hisperica Famina*, "Western utterances" (or perhaps "Latin verses"), which take their title from the *explicit* of a poem, some 600 lines long, as it appears in the principal MS. containing it (Cod. Vat. Reg. Latin 81)—"Hisperica finiunt famina."

This piece was first printed, from the Vatican text, by Cardinal Mai in 1832 (*Class. Auct.* v, p. 479, Migne, *P.L.* xc, col. 1185). He did not recognize it as verse, or at least was content to leave it as he found it written in continuous prose.

Bradshaw, happening upon it in Mai when he was looking for something else, noticed at once that the sentences were rhythmical, each containing one or more pairs of rhyming or assonant words, an adjective in the middle and a substantive at the end. He began a lineal arrangement, and a pencil note, printed in *Collected Papers*, p. 463, gives a specimen which, as he said, conveys a better idea of the rhythm than any verbal explanation:

> Cibonea : pliadum non exhomicant fulgora.
> merseum solifluus : eruit neuum tractus.
> densos phetoneum : extricat sudos incendium.
> roscida : aret rubigine stillicidia.
> nec oliuatus frondea : oliuat nimbus robora.
> faenosas : diuiduat imber uuas.
> micras uricomus : apricat lacunas rogus.
> mundanum : que torret iubar girum[1].

[1] The reader may fairly ask what all this means, and as F. J. is not here to stop me I venture to offer an approximate rendering:
"The food-giving beams of the Pleiades flash not forth;
The sweep of rays streaming from the sun overthrows the dusky night;
The blaze of Phaethon scatters the thick clouds;
The drops of dew dry up under the sun's rust;
Nor doth the dark cloud hide the leafy oaks;
The rain-cloud forsakes the glistering grapes;
The pyre with golden tresses (reading *auricomus*) warms the little pools;
And the sun's beam scorches the circle of the earth."
In any case it is a description of the effects of sunrise.

Bradshaw knew all about it, was able to construe the whole thing, had decided its provenance[1], intended to issue it with a commentary, and at his death only needed a fortnight to have it ready for press.

This was in itself a kind of challenge which Jenkinson was encouraged to take up by Henry Jackson.

I do not know the exact date when he began to play with this poem, but it was certainly long before 1895 when he notes in his Diary *s.d.* Feb. 5: "began work at Hisp. Fam." This beginning had unexpected external stimulus. He tells his sister in May, 1895:

I have been much interested and excited by receiving from Prof. Zimmer of Greinwald some work which carries on Bradshaw's discoveries in relation to the Hisperica Famina ("Western utterances"), poems in extraordinary corrupt, artificial Latin, written perhaps in the 6th or 7th century in some Celtic district. I have been pottering over the subject, and could have added one or two poems, if I had known he was about it.

Work on *Hisperica Famina* meant for Jenkinson writing out the lines after Bradshaw's model, making an index of words, much consulting of glossaries and contemporary literature, and especially a minute examination of the Cambridge MS. Gg. 5.35 which provides Hisperic material. Texts A and B were fully written out by May, 1897. The fruits of his long familiarity are a critical edition, published in 1908, comprising four texts of the main poem (of which one is a series of glosses, and two are fragments) together with other relevant pieces, the well-known *Lorica* of Gildas, the Hymn "Adelphus adelpha" and the *Rubisca*, hitherto unpublished.

For the Vatican MS. upon which he chiefly depended Jenkinson had the invaluable help of the late H. M. Bannister who collated for him on the spot; the Paris fragments were sent over by M. Léopold Delisle; the Cambridge MS. supplied the *Rubisca*, the *Adelphus*, and other miscellanea.

To the texts he prefixed an introduction of forty pages de-

[1] "It is by an Irishman."

scribing the MSS., and briefly indicating the main peculiarities of Hisperic syntax and vocabulary, and the volume closes with an exhaustive *index verborum*.

What is wanting to render an edition for which such preparation was made, and which was so carefully carried out, complete and definitive? A translation, or at least a commentary, which the editor was most eminently capable of supplying.

Definitive it is for the text; complete it is as far as Jenkinson meant to go. But he said,

I do not feel that like Bradshaw I can construe the whole. And where the meaning of a word does not come home to me, I prefer to leave others to pursue the investigation without prejudice or infelicitous suggestion to lead them from the right way.

This apology hides a tacit protest against the edition of J. M. Stowasser (1887) which, besides retaining the unintelligent prose arrangement of Mai, was marred, in spite of much learning, by rash conjecture. Jenkinson's copy is punctuated with notes of admiration and laconic remarks in the manner of Malherbe upon Desportes.

The student of literature must regret the extreme fastidiousness which withheld the help he certainly needs for reading the *Hisperica Famina*, but the student of character will admit that this little work is in keeping with all we know of Jenkinson. Here is not only a true scholar's modesty and scrupulous accuracy (Titivillius the demon who prompts to misprints was thoroughly worsted for once!) but a clarity of exposition and a sensitiveness to beauty even in unpromising surroundings which was his in an especial degree. For instance, on the clause "multiformis solifluis: pretenui nubium uapore stemicatur arcus radiis,"[1] he comments:

Such a line as that which I have quoted is very remarkable: and we are left to wonder how such a vocabulary came to be associated with such artistic feeling. It is not enough to suppose that behind the Latin expression may stand thoughts conceived

[1] Perhaps "The rainbow is decked with varied rays streaming from the sun on the translucent mist of clouds."

in native Irish. That seems likely enough. But, apart from that, there is a directness and freedom in the expression itself which, as far as I know, cannot be matched among other remnants of contemporary literature.

He who can perceive and write like that is more than a mere scholar and antiquary.

As to the ultimate value of the *Hisperica Famina* upon which Jenkinson spent so much trouble and in which he found aesthetic pleasure, it is usual to rate it very low. M. Roger apologizes for having to deal with such rubbish; Teuffel dubs it "foolish cant and occult language of the Scottish monks"; Rhys describes it as "a kind of rhythmic twaddle about astronomy and the prophet in the lions' den." An eminent living mediaevalist has expressed to me his regret that Jenkinson wasted his time on "that exasperating product of human folly and bad taste." The obvious reply to which remark is that taste varies and that the story of humanity is in general the story of man's folly. For the rest it is enough to say that matter which engaged the interest of Bradshaw and Henry Jackson and M. R. James[1] and Francis Jenkinson may not be dismissed with a sneer.

[1] Cf. *Cambridge Medieval History*, vol. III, p. 507.

Chapter X

RECREATIONS

SUCH was Jenkinson at work. We have now to consider his recreations and relaxations, or rather, the pursuits which he followed, outside the Library, during the last half of his life with the same youthful zest that marked all his actions.

First, undoubtedly, comes music; not that he spent most time on it, but because of the intensity of his enjoyment.

He was never a performer, and it is perhaps as well, for an instrument would have absorbed more energy than he could spare. But the small skill which he had on the piano gave him occasional satisfaction, though his fingers, so adroit with the forceps, were clumsy on the notes. Thus, he writes, after a visit to Hubert Parry's home in 1885, "I have got some small Preludes by Bach, which Dolly used to play, while I was dressing, at Rustington; and I amuse myself by going through them, rather slowly, but with some pleasure." And, in 1897, "The night before last I solemnly ploughed through the fugue at the end of Brahms's Handel variations; just to remind me of the notes"; and he would sometimes put in the voice part with one hand when the pianist was fully occupied with the accompaniment.

He did not sing, as men count singing; but, like the nephew of Rameau whom Diderot describes in a famous passage, he could reproduce by lips and gesture, whistling and humming and beating time, the whole effect of an orchestra[1]. Jenkinson had the imitative gift without the delirious extravagances which

---

[1] "Il rendait les cors et les bassons; il prenait un son éclatant et nasillard pour les hautbois; précipitant sa voix avec une rapidité incroyable pour les instruments à cordes dont il cherchait les sons les plus approchés...il sifflait les petites flûtes, il roucoulait les traversières, criant, chantant, se démenant comme un forcené, faisant lui seul les chanteurs, les chanteuses, tout un orchestre, tout un théâtre lyrique, et se divisant en vingt rôles."

Diderot's exuberant pen attributes to his hero. Like him "he mastered the soul of his hearers and kept them spell-bound," infecting them with his enthusiasm. And to sit beside him at a concert when the strings were sounding was to be transported into another sphere. He would lean across and flutter his fingers on the shoulder of a more phlegmatic hearer when a passage occurred which especially excited him, his face beaming with delight. No one knew better how to listen to music, and he did his best to make others hear with his ears and his intelligence. To a girl (Miss M. C. Stewart) who was beginning the musician's pilgrimage *via* St James's Hall he wrote in the winter of 1880:

I must...call your attention to the Monday Popular Concert tomorrow night. If you can possibly go to hear Schubert's Octett you ought to do so. It is one of the most beautiful things ever written—especially abounding in lovely passages for horns, which are so exquisitely touching. You should be in the Balcony (3s.) *facing* the Orchestra. Do manage it and let me know your impressions, and then I shall have something to console me for not being there....As last Monday was such a success, I must tell you that next Monday is again an unusually good programme. The Mozart Quartett is one of his most melodious and touching; and Schumann's Quintett ranks among the best works of the kind in existence. It is an unceasing course of exquisite tunes from beginning to end: each movement is a masterpiece, with a perfect overflow of materials succeeding one another in lavish profusion. I shall send you a little score, which you can use to follow with: but don't be a slave to it or you will not be able to enjoy the music so well. Look it over first and know the lie of the ground, but if you lose your place, wait till the end of the movement. The Octett is indeed a beautiful work; you must have enlarged your ideas as to the capabilities of horns, and have I hope some charming recollections. I shall hope to find you at home some day after I come down; and then we will talk over what you have heard.

Concerning another he writes:

....gave ——— some advice about music and the need of listening attentively (comparing a picture moved across a screen): she said it had never struck her before; and so it is with most people: they never notice that in the first place you cannot look at a musical composition *all at once*, and secondly you cannot ever look at *a bit of it* long enough to take it in without concentrated attention or exceptional receptivity. (April 1, 1883.)

It is evident that what the Germans call *Einfühlung* and the English psychologists "Empathy" (a doubtful Graecism), *i.e.* the capacity, common to all simple and generous natures, of projecting into others, who are innocent of them, feelings and sensations of your own, was developed in Jenkinson to an unusual degree. He could not imagine that any one of whom he was fond for other reasons could fail to be moved by what appealed to him. Thus to E. G. Duff whose *forte* in music was harmless humorous songs he exclaims, "Do go and hear the Ninth Symphony on Wednesday afternoon. It would be a comfort to know you are there, if I am not." It was the same with all his hobbies—insects, books, flowers, even the *Hisperica Famina*. "B— (a country gentleman) looked in and I shewed him the *Hisperica Famina* in which he took an intelligent interest; and quite saw the point of them."

Although that particular gift of the gods, a sense of perfect pitch, was denied him, his ear was extraordinarily accurate and he was quick to detect a false intonation. He once had a passage of arms with Stanford at a performance of the Beethoven Violin Concerto in 1886. Jenkinson said the kettledrums were out of tune. Stanford said they were not; a heated argument ensued which greatly amused Joachim. The event is chronicled in Jo.'s handwriting by a "Timpani ♩ ♩ ♩ ♩" on the frame of his shadow-picture, drawn by Herkomer in 1881 for Jenkinson, which had a fresh inscription added at each of his visits to Cambridge. When he came, there were always festive celebrations in his honour in college, or later at Trumpington Hall, or at Madingley Rise, and Jenkinson was the life and soul of them. He used to recount with glee how he managed to procure a special performance of the Schumann Fantasia (Op. 121). It was on this wise. Miss Geraldine Liddell had told him that she once sat beside Joachim at a dinner the fish course of which was

fresh herrings. Jo. turned to her and said, "My favor-rite fish."
Jenkinson remembered this and in 1879—but let him tell the
story himself in a letter which admits us to a share of his youthful
musical enthusiasm (he was only twenty-five), and of his happy
intimacy with the great violinist.

Cambridge, March 18 [1879].

My dear Nelly,

    I cannot keep up with all I ought to tell you.

    Last Monday (Jan. (*sic*) 10)...I again went to London, not
so much for the Pop. as to see Mrs Liddell, who was staying
at 68 Cornwall Gardens; and on Tuesday, after the Bach Choir,
I went there to tea with her and Mary, and staid till 9.15, when
I had to run for my train. She was looking so plump and well,
you would hardly have known her; of course I had a very happy
evening. Franco has taken to chemical works in default of
engineer employment. She and Edward went north on Saturday.
At the Pop. were with me Benson and Mr Hudson, the 'cello
player, who had arrived at King's X from Yorkshire just in
front of me[1]. The Schumann Fantasia was thoroughly good, with
lovely arpeggio passages, etc. Well, when Thursday came, I had
caught a creepy cold, and shivered over the fire all day, and
half thought the concert must go. But I screwed myself together
and went, and survived, but in poor condition—no headache
however. We had the Schumann A minor Quartett, three
familiar *Stücke im Volkston*, Viotti's Adagio and 2 Hungarian
Dances and a Bach Solo (as an encore):

 etc.

Then the Beethoven C$\sharp$ minor Quartett. All I can say is that
some parts are catching and delightful at once, and some in-
telligibly beautiful; but a great deal seems at first hearing not
only ugly, but aimless; so be prepared for a hard listen on the 2nd.
More would be of no use till you have heard it. At supper I
presided at the end remote from Jo.; but was charmed with
Ries, to whom the name of Liddell was an introduction: and

---

[1] The *dramatis personae* of the first paragraphs are Mrs Edward Liddell,
her sister Miss Mary Fraser-Tytler (now Mrs G. F. Watts), Franco their
brother, Mr Robin Benson, Mr Percy Hudson (better known as Canon
Percy Pemberton).

we talked about various things, including Mlle Janotha, but I must keep that till we meet. They all smoked, and when I went to bed, I was quite dazed. I woke with an excruciating headache, and sent to have my place at dinner filled up. However about 3 o'clock I found the pain was gone, and so I got up; and at 9 I dressed and went to the Stanfords, and came in just as they were in the drawing-room. Now it had occurred to me the day before to tell Mrs Stanford of Jo.'s love for herrings, and so she had some, and when he saw them, he simply beamed, and wondered how she knew. So afterwards she produced me as the source of her information, and he was so nice about it, and said what a memory I must have for *great* things! and when his turn came to play, I begged for the Schumann Fantaisie of Monday last, and he said I should have it as a reward for the herrings. Fancy standing within two yards as he played it: it was even better on a second hearing, and Mr Hudson, who rather made light of it on Monday, amended his opinion, which was what I most wanted. Afterwards, as we talked about it, Jo. naïvely remarked, "It is very difficult to play," the fact being that it was written for him, and hardly anybody else could play it at all. Soon he found a heap of Schubert Songs about, and to make Mrs Stanford sing one she didn't know, he sat down and played and hummed it; such a touch, and such feeling in his voice and face: he cannot manage his fingers on the piano always, but what he can do, is far away from all common players. The song was "Dass du hier gewesen" —it begins

etc.

When we came away, I ventured to ask by what train he went by next morning, and finding it suited me, I arranged that my cab should take us both (you know we *Fellows* have cabs into the College) and so I went with him to London, talking about many things most of the way. He wanted to know what "weird" meant, and so I had to think of instances to tell him, and I think he understood. I am told "unheimlich" is the word for it. Then we drove to St James's Hall and as there was an hour before his rehearsal for the Saturday Pop., he asked me to come up to their room, where he put in a string and proceeded to practise fiendish scales and passages, with his eyes shut, going over some things dozens of times. I staid with him nearly an hour, and then we said good-bye and after lunch with Aunt Augusta I went to the Crystal Palace, where I had been given a stall, to hear the Eroica. The first movement is what you can guess; the Trio is nearly all Horns—divine. Now I must send this off: so good-bye.

It was perhaps the excitement of these reminiscences which caused him to drop his signature and give a wrong date!

Nearly all his knowledge of the art of music (and it came to be profound) was picked up by him as he went along in the way indicated by this delightful epistle. He knew his way about a score, although he could not read it like a trained musician to whom the written page speaks as plainly as the performance. He never studied harmony systematically, nor did exercises in counterpoint, nor tried to compose. But he had an instinctive feeling, fostered by acute and assiduous listening, for what was right whether according to rule, or by the more exacting canons of taste. There is a "thirteenth" in the last line of Dykes's popular hymn, "The King of Love my Shepherd is," aggravated by a monotonous "pedal," which caused him physical discomfort: "a horrid squirm in the tenor" he called it. And he would often protest against a chord as wrong even if he could not tell you why. I remember his maintaining stoutly, against Mr Fuller-Maitland, the unsuitable "modernity" of a harmony in Stanford's setting of "The flight of the Earls." But he could give no reason.

He was particularly interested in rhythm and was restless until he understood the metre of a piece. There is a little "exercise" in the Fitzwilliam Book in three-part counterpoint without clef or time-signature which was an endless source of inquiry and perplexity to him. But his musical judgement even though entirely intuitive, was greatly valued by masters of the art who are gone—Hubert Parry, "my beloved Hubert," Grove, Parratt, Stanford—and by many who remain. He was elected

¹ Professor Stanford sent him a post-card: "Oct. 18, '17. Sedley (*i.e.* Sedley Taylor) has resigned the Chairmanship of the Musical Board. I pray you for all our sakes to consent to fill his place. There is next to nothing to do, but to keep a kindly but firm hand at the very few meetings. And you of all men are the man to do that. C. V. S."

Chairman of the Musical Board at Cambridge (partly no doubt for his eirenical qualities) in 1917 and held the office till his death.

It would be an exaggeration to say that Jenkinson's taste in music was catholic. He was an impenitent conservative, and post-Victorian (and some Victorian) developements whether in England or abroad found as a rule little favour with him.

Of Debussy he notes in 1908:

Dent played a good deal of Debussy's *Pelléas et Mélisande* which is full of beauty and interested us very much.

And in 1912:

Some Debussy is worth hearing, when you are fresh.

On the other hand in 1923 we find,

Borwick Concert. Bach, Mozart, Beethoven, Brahms (Paganini Variations). I enjoyed it all but the first Debussy which was the usual dreary lingo.

And this probably represents his definitive opinion.

An "All-English" performance at Cambridge in 1887 is severely judged:

The Orchestral concert of English composers was exhausting; *The Revenge* was a relief; I had not heard it before. I don't care for the Mackenzie Violin Concerto, nor for Cowen's Symphony. It seems all waste, aimless striving with no meaning.

But the Festival of British Music organized by the C.U.M.S. in 1922 with Eccles's *Masque of Venus* and two eighteenth-century operas and Vaughan Williams's ballet of Old King Cole gave him great pleasure.

The dialect was one which he did not comprehend; he found it ugly and tiring. "The Ravel exhausted me, so I read proofs." Once he went to tea with a musical undergraduate whose teacher played Bach, Beethoven—and then Ravel. Jenkinson grew whiter and whiter and at last, saying half aloud, "I'm afraid I can't stand it; I must go," he bolted.

Even Wagner he could not away with. He dismissed the *Siegfried Idyll* as morbid—it was one of his pet aversions—and when he heard that a friend had fallen sick at Bayreuth he said, "*Tristan* perhaps" (it proved to be typhoid).

He loved Vaughan Williams, the man and his *Wasps* and his setting of folk-songs and *The Sea Symphony* as far as he could follow it; but his *London Symphony* deafened him, and he said plaintively in hospital at Holloway, "I am having a London Symphony of my own here with busses and clanging trams and street noises."

His veneration for J. S. Bach was profound, but he did not subscribe to the indiscriminating and exclusive cult which he saw rising of later years. His chief hero was Beethoven—everyone *must* hear the Ninth Symphony and *Fidelio* and the Mass in D, which I really believe he preferred to the B minor Mass because of its immense humanity. After Beethoven perhaps Brahms. "I have no doubt that Brahms is the great man of this generation," he wrote in 1875, and his was a generation which in its turn paid to Brahms the same kind of homage which the great Saxon enjoys today. Then came Schubert and Schumann, Chopin of the Etudes and Preludes and Mazurkas, the "fairy" music of Mendelssohn—though on the whole he preferred Sterndale Bennett—and later under the influence of his wife, Mozart and Haydn and the old Frenchmen, Couperin and Rameau, and Purcell and the Elizabethans of the Virginals Book. For Handel except his *Semele*, he had but scant respect.

One of his early operatic experiences is of interest if only as shewing the material from which his mature taste was formed:

July 25, 1876....I have actually heard 3 operas, and as I think, as good a trio as could be put together: Faust, Fidelio, and Don Giovanni. Faust was quite charming, and I remember more of it than of the others. Faure as Mephistopheles sang the Serenade with the most diabolic and bewitching air, and I have never been able to get him out of my head since.

I heard the overture to Fidelio, and Leonora no. 3, which last was encored....I have got the music of Fidelio, so we can look through it together.

Don Giovanni was the most delightful mixture of comic and tragic. Masetto and Leporello are quite ludicrous all through—and fancy Titiens, Nielsen and Trebelli-Bettini all at once.

The interpreters by whom he measured all late comers were Madame Schumann, Joachim, Hausmann, Mühlfeld, Faure, Sims Reeves, Miss Fillunger, von Zur Mühlen; and among amateurs R. C. Rowe, Miss Lucy Frere (now Mrs Barnes) for Schubert and Brahms songs; his wife for Mozart and the old masters; and for general musicianship, Miss G. M. Liddell[1].

All these assertions are borne out by his Journal from which I cull the following additional *obiter scripta*:

1881, Jan. 3. "Dvořák 4tett, German band dash, rowdy." (He appreciated some of the Bohemian composer's music, but not his *Spectre's Bride* nor the *New World Symphony*.)

1894, June 13. "*Messiah* at King's. It satisfies me even less than I expected; merely profane, most of it."

1897, Feb. 3. "German has some stuff in him and is melodious and can hold on through some stiffish modulations. But there is too much undigested Wagner, etc. Jos. Reed sang without affectation, much better to hear than Edward Lloyd."

1900, Feb. 13 (of some quartet). "A good deal of pleasure, but they are not so *conscientious* as Joachim, and began the Schumann too fast."

1904, Nov. 16. "Kruse 4tet played Schumann Op. 41 badly and Beethoven Op. 74 very well. Meta Diestel sang Hugo Wolf, Schumann, Schubert, and Brahms beautifully. It was quite a red letter day."

1904, Nov. 17. "Lamb had been with Kruse, etc. last night. K. thought they played the Schumann well, better than the Beethoven, and he did not like the singing. Such are professionals."

1906, March 7. "The Schumann Fantasia did not please us at all, partly owing to the piano, partly because not played simply and broadly."

---

[1] I am tempted to add the name of Ronald McKenzie, once of the 78th Highlanders and afterwards piper to the Duke of Richmond, for Jenkinson's Scotch blood thrilled to the bag-pipes and he admitted such things as The McIntosh's and McCrimmon's Laments to the category of real music. When the cadets were at Trinity during the War, Ronald's son "Sandy" played round the High Table with grand effect.

1906, Nov. 19. "Some Bach (Sheffield Choir) very un-satisfactory—wearisome noise as heard by us."

1908, Dec. 29. "—— did not make the Beethoven speak, and even the *Humoreske* was not at all as Mme Schumann played it. Jerky and violent and lacking in poetry."

1909, Oct. 21. "*Mot* by one of the Wasps' orchestra over-heard: 'This is the stuff for me: none of your d—d tonic and dominant.'"

1911, Jan. 26. "A splendid programme and Borsdorff, Malsch, Davies, etc. in the orchestra. —— as a conductor is effective, but rather coarse and blatant, and if he has any reverence for Beethoven or insight, it does not appear. He has a tiresome gesture with his left hand, a kind of flip, which is almost vulgar."

1912, June 6. "*Sea Symphony*. It seemed to be fine stuff, very expressive, though I could not always understand it."

1919, June 19 [working in the Bodleian]. "Meanwhile close by, a great rehearsal of "Blest Pair of Sirens" and V. W.'s *Sea Symphony* was distracting my attention and making me wish I could stay."

After music, flies. Entomology was perhaps his earliest passion. His father used to tell how the little fellow, when he could hardly speak, would stand on the hearth-rug opposite a case of moths, wriggling his shoulders and crying, "Caddy to see moffs!" Reference to the account of his school days in this volume will shew how the taste was fostered and, his school and college friends still remember his zeal as a collector of moths and butterflies. The late Mr Nelson M. Richardson who was at Trinity with him writes:

In those days he used to be very keen about collecting *Micro-lepidoptera* and my chief memories of him are associated with our joint expeditions to Wicken Fen and elsewhere which I greatly enjoyed and profited by, as his knowledge of these beautiful and delicate little creatures was much greater than mine.... He was always a pleasant companion and his methods and ideas were interesting and often entertaining. If he caught one specimen of even a rare species he would remark that it was common; when he obtained a second, he said that it swarmed, and if a third was captured, he pronounced it to be a pest! when others such as myself would have been only too glad to get a fourth or more.

Mr E. Meyrick says:

I believe I had no particular friendship with Jenkinson at Marlborough; he was in my house, etc., but a year above me in standing, and at Marlborough those of the same year generally associated together. I feel sure I never went out collecting with him, for instance.... It was when I went up to Cambridge that we became very friendly; then I was often in his rooms, and we collected together in the season two or three days a week, particularly at Madingley and Cherry Hinton chalk-pits which proved inexhaustible mines of interest, and also made excursions. On such special occasions I remember generally that breakfast previously in his rooms meant that I had breakfast comfortably while he could be heard scrambling up in the next room, and finally snatching a hasty mouthful with the responsibility thrown on me of saying when he must absolutely start to catch the train. Notwithstanding his real enthusiasm he dropped collecting when I left, for want of a companion[1]. At the time when he took his degree, his constitution (of which he was always careless, being very irregular in his habits[2]) had been much overstrained, and these collecting walks would have been good for him. They were in abeyance until he took up *Diptera* many years later.... If he had possessed the energy to take up some definite scientific line and run it independently, he had every ability requisite to make a first-class success. He ought to have been a man of science. He had every qualification needed for a microlepidopterous student, and really they are rarely found in combination.

A letter to his sister of August 16, 1876, gives a vivid picture of his entomological zeal when Mr Meyrick was there to foster it:

Thanks very much for your prompt reply with the Thrift. To my delight this morning, as I looked into my pot of thrift-heads I found a lovely *Tortrix, unknown to me,* which had

---

[1] It is certainly true that his power of initiation was inferior to his accomplishment. As he said *à propos* of his success in pinning flies, "It shews how easy it is to do a thing when some one gives you a lead."

[2] Cf. "Last night at 12 o'clock just as I was coming away from Piggott to go to bed, in walked Turner, and we sat there reading Shakespeare, etc. for $6\frac{1}{2}$ hours: when I went to bed, but they did not. We all agreed that it was worth doing once in a way, and I feel none the worse." And there are notes of other sittings late into the morning, which may have been all very well for the others, but for a delicate creature like Jenkinson were wicked. However, if he had looked after himself he would not have been himself.

appeared unbeknown like—I supposed all the larvae were Brizella. I hope *some* are still, although I find the larvae of Brizella (I don't know where this blot came from) ought to be feeding 6 weeks hence. Today just in time to save one of my eight larvae, Circaea has turned up in Humphrey's garden, and a stunted plant which I did not see before in the Bot. Gardens, so I hope *he* will live. If you are in any wood where the plant grows, look out for the mines like Catherine wheels and send them me in a tin box. I should so like a good series of them, lovely orange moths with silvery markings. An old Barn Owl is screeching about in the Backs. Meyrick was away a month and brought back 600 specimens of micros, new to him, and 300 big things. In South France he could not venture out at midday for the heat; in the Engadine it snowed hard! The Thermometer here minimizes about 70°. Yesterday afternoon the pot boiled over, and the lobsters breathed freely, *i.e.* there was a really violent thunderstorm—one crack exploded close to us in the cloisters like a charge of blasting-powder as far as the sound went, startling us nearly out of our shoes. I never heard anything like it before, and a fellow near us felt a distinct shock, and a taste in his mouth. The afternoon before I had a tremendous hunt after a CAMBERWELL BEAUTY!!!!!!! I was hunting a willow tree just behind the Library, when he started from close to my head, and floating quietly away, settled 25 feet up the Library wall. I got a ladder, but missed him; he flew off and settled about 6 feet above a ledge which ran along about 6 feet up. I could not get any hold, so we moved the ladder to where there was a ring by which I pulled myself on to the ledge and walked along. He was in a nasty corner and I missed him again. He then settled right on the top, and I was going to get the key to go on to the roof, when an inquisitive sparrow started him and he disappeared! Every one looked out next morning, and a friend of mine named Bull[1] eventually caught it with my net on the same tree where I started it, of which it seemed very fond. It is unlucky, but I am glad somebody has it. It is a peculiarly fine specimen, but a little rubbed. I found two Eyed Hawk caterpillars on the same willow tree. The above-mentioned Bull, nephew of C. M. Bull, wants me to go to Skye with him for the first fortnight of Sept. for sea-trout fishing: he stays at the inn at Sligachan. Of course I should like to, but can't. Could Charlie? as Bull jumped at the

[1] Now the Rev. H. A. Bull.

idea and the enthusiasm *in re piscatoria* would be a bond of union.

As Mr Meyrick says, he laid aside the practice of entomology from his college days until a fateful morning in February, 1900, when his Diary notes among other things: "Dr Sharp came in with a lovely box of *Diptera* from the New Forest." This fired the train, and from then till the end (his first action on going into his hospital ward was to catch—and lose—a *Musca domestica*) the collecting of all sorts of flies went on, by net and by hand. He had a mantis-like agility in catching them in his fingers or with one of the glass-topped receptacles which filled his pockets. "*Culex fasciatus* settled on the bridge of my nose: boxed it," runs one entry. This extraordinary feat will surprise the reader less when he learns that Jenkinson could leap into the air and snap a hovering fly into one of his pill-boxes.

He began at Nairn and at Logie House near Forres whither he went on holiday in August that year, pursued by consignments of apparatus from Dr Sharp, who had now caught him as surely as one of his own specimens. By September 11 he was back in Cambridge, and having summoned Sharp to luncheon and coming in late himself he found him gloating over the prizes of a short month's activity. A fortnight later they were all pinned and named to the number of several hundreds.

His eyes were opened afresh to the good and bad habits of the insect world. On a hot September day he lay out all the morning at Logie:

Watched the wasp-colony by the ash tree beside the drive. One was excavating nearly all the time, throwing out soil about every 3 minutes. Sometimes he went off, probably for food. Latterly he began putting his head out and drawing earth, etc. *back* into the hole. I saw one of them eating a house-fly on my plaid; and twice I saw a biggish fly (two sorts) brought in to store. The second time the wasp was below his hole, and found the fly too heavy: he then climbed a leaf to get a better take off: I looked away for a moment and he must have got in then. A ♂ (*Conops quadri-fasciatus*) bearing up for the colony looked so like a smallish common wasp that I felt obliged to catch it to be sure what it was, and so lost the chance of watching it. A ♀ at the *spiraea* I missed, having no net. An ant was dragging off a small *green* bug, with a *red* acarus on it; very gay.

In parenthesis. I think there is no doubt that like that great entomologist Charles Oberthür, the chief attraction for Jenkinson in the creatures which he caught was the beauty of their form, shape, colour and habits[1].

But the record sometimes reads less romantically. Back at Cambridge on October 1 (1900), he notes:

Found the flies in the grocer's shop belonged to cheese (*Piophila casei*); and the ♀s were hard at work ovipositing, pushing their tails in. I remarked that the cheese would soon be full of maggots. "Oh!" said the grocer, "it will all be sold before that!"

The next year, when he collected at Hindon (Wilts), in the New Forest, and again in the North, was signalized among other trophies by the capture of a species new to science (named by him *Brachypeza radiata*) on the window of his little green-house in Cambridge. His household was enlisted in the cause. Annie Allard, the cook, was a first-rate observer and a nimble collector, and both she and the housemaid presently had their own collection pinned on squares and dated.

His contribution to the literature of the subject consists of twenty-three short notes and papers in *The Entomologist's Monthly Magazine*. In the longest of these, "Notes on certain Mycetophilidae" (1908), he records and describes sixteen species of fungus gnat (besides the one already mentioned) apparently new to Britain. There are also many new species discovered by him but described by others, and he has the honour of being gossip to one named by Mr F. W. Edwards, *Sciophila jenkinsoni*. His work in connexion with fungus gnats is handsomely acknowledged by Mr Edwards in what is still the standard paper on the subject[2]. The inclusion of *Culex apicalis* in the list of British

[1] Cf. the obituary notice of C. O. (d. June, 1924) by N. D. R(iley) in *The Entomologist*, vol. LVII, no. 735, p. 192.

[2] Cf. "Notes on British Mycetophilidae," by F. W. Edwards, *Trans. of the Entom. Society* for 1913, pp. 334–382.

mosquitoes depends on a single example taken at Logie by Jenkinson, who also caught at Crowborough the remarkable scaly-winged *Copeognathe* (Psocid) described by Enderlein as a new genus and species—*Pteroxanium squamosum*[1].

He shewed rare skill in mounting the tiny creatures, and his pleasure in displaying them was infectious. His wife describes the process:

"Oh I hate flies, nasty things," someone would say, and he would reply by gently leading the speaker to a table on which stood a wooden box and a microscope and extract from the box a minute object impaled on a tiny pin, which he would gently place beneath the microscope[2] and the ignoramus would be led to a chair beside the table and invited to look through the microscope while the lenses were carefully adjusted. And then the ecstatic ejaculations would cause his face to kindle with glee and delight. "Isn't it lovely?" he would say. "But now wait one moment and I will shew you something more wonderful still." He never got tired of these exhibitions or impatient of any ignorance; he simply loved to share the beauties of his treasures with every one."[3]

An extract from a letter of June 6, 1905, shews him in the full flush of his collecting enthusiasm, at work in his favourite hunting-grounds:

I was doing rather well those two or three hot days. On the 29th Sharp and I started from a meeting at Jackson's about 6 p.m. First, at a hole in a lime in Trinity Avenue we found a number of *Psychodas* (those little flies like bats or moths) of a kind we do not know. Then behind Clare, on a decrepit elm are some big yellow funguses. I have often looked at them: but at last, on that day we saw a lot of little black flies sitting on their under surface. I had slippery boots, and felt I could not get up: but a boy coming from bathing lent me his towel to throw up, and as it stuck, we shoved him up to get it, and then I thought he

---

[1] Cf. Dr Hugh Scott's obituary notices of his friend in *Nature* for October 6, 1923, p. 516, and in the *Ent. Monthly Mag.* vol. LIX, pp. 261–262. Dr Scott tells me that this insect has since been rediscovered in the Bristol district and in North Wales.

[2] The gift of Horace Darwin, all the more treasured for the sake of the donor.

[3] Cf. *A Fragrance of Sweet Memories*, by M. C. Jenkinson, privately printed (1924).

might as well try with a tube to secure a sample. He succeeded perfectly. It proved to be a very rare *Platypeza* (*P. furcata*), which I *have* found in the garden, but Verrall only records it on two specimens from Herefordshire. I also caught with my hand, hovering, a very odd sun-fly, I have only once taken, at Logie. Then we found a fallen elm, sawn into lengths: the sawn surface was very attractive, and we caught a few things, but our only boxes were full. On the 31st I went round again and there were the flies again. I went up with two tubes, and caught *nine*! The elm was entirely cleaved away. A decayed willow on Sheep's Green on which I had a short time ago got a fungus beetle (*Engis humeralis*) had its fungus swollen by rain in the night; and I got six more of them, to Sharp's delight. So you see I was having a rather good time. And on Saturday in the garden I got about 40 things, some rather good.

Men of science were fortunate in having at the head of the University Library one of their own clan who was sympathetic to their needs, and a classical scholar able to help in the right formation of scientific names; and the entomologists of Cambridge must always be grateful to the memory of him who put the pick of his captures at the disposal of the University Museum and directed that when he left this scene all his vast collection should go there just as his coins went to the Fitzwilliam, and such of his books as were wanted to the Library and to Trinity.

The benefit which Jenkinson derived from his pursuit of flies in the open air was probably lessened by the strain of mounting them under the microscope. But he had other occupations to tempt him out of doors. He had been something of a sportsman in his youth. He was a good skater and regarded hockey on the ice as a game for kings. He had gone fly-fishing with Duff in the 'nineties, and he had shot along shore and in covert at Scilly as late as 1901.

At Cambridge he practically lived in his garden when not in the Library. When he went out of College (he was an active member of the committee in charge of the grounds) he made the most of the strip of poor soil behind his house in Brookside where he had a small green-house, the gift of W. H. Macaulay, filled it with mesembrianthemums and sweet-scented geraniums:

AT AUCHENBOWIE   1905

AT AUCHENBOWIE   1905

here, too, lived and were lost and recovered a pair of tree-frogs from the Riviera. And on moving to Chaucer Road (1907) with its acre of ground he carried with him for their own or for association's sake many precious plants, which like their master flourished in the better surroundings. There he built a larger green-house, sunk a rockery, and met with the success which his paternal tending of his plants deserved.

One piece of practical advice to timid pruners may be quoted: "You must fix your attention on what you leave and never mind what you cut away."

I am indebted to Mr H. Gilbert Carter, Director of the University Botanic Garden for the following note:

He was first a botanist, then a gardener. I was once with him in his garden, when his lynx-eye detected a strange plant on one of the beds. It proved to be *Chenopodium vulvaria*, a foetid weed with small green flowers. Many so-called gardeners think so much of colour that they are nearly blind to form. Jenkinson was not one of these. To him *Chenopodium vulvaria* was no mere weed; he knew its individuality, its leaf form, its intrinsic beauty. We brought it into the house, and I read to him from Ascherson-Graebner's *Flora des Nordostdeutschen Flachlandes*: "Der höchst unangenehme Geruch dieser Pflanze rührt von Trimethylamin her, demselben Stoff, der auch in der Heringslake vorkommt." I was surprised to learn that he knew some Organic Chemistry, and was familiar with trimethylamine.

The beauty of his garden resulted from his love of plants. The plants at Southmead that we remember so well were not horticulturists' varieties, but natural species. Why so many of them throve so luxuriantly it is not easy to say. He sedulously covered the roots of his *Daphne Blagayana* with stones, a practice recommended in books on gardening. His *Olearia insignis*[1] grew in a frame, which protected it from frost. But most of his memorable plants, for example his *Rosa Moyesii*, luxuriated for no particular reason.

They grew large and beautiful in the refulgence of his affection. There is much in the Second Part of Shelley's *Sensitive Plant* that helps us to understand the connexion between

[1] This fine plant was grown from seed sent to him from Scilly in 1912. It was one of his special favourites and he had it photographed more than once. It now flourishes in the Botanic Garden.

Jenkinson and his garden. Many will carry with them to the end the memory of the keen joy of being in that garden with him; only those know what a plant meant to him who could collate the keenness of his eye with the refinement of his mind.

No account of Jenkinson in his garden would be complete without reference to his incessant warfare against weeds of all sorts and in all places, especially against *Agrostis stolonifera* which Bentham and Hooker describe as "an elegant grass" but which he regarded as a pestilent usurper and was quite as eager to expel from the Bowling Green at Trinity as from his own lawn. He would follow its endless ramifications with inexorable fingers after ruffling the turf with his open hand "to make the brute stand up," and then carry off the spoil to the bonfire whose fitful play of smoke and flame exercised on him the same fascination as the eddies and currents of a highland stream.

He was a first-rate field naturalist. Reference has already been made to his observation of migrants, astonishing to the cockney, and to the story of the Andalusian Quail, which turned out to be a Virginian. His real addition to ornithological history is his record of the second (if not the first) occurrence of the American Kildeer Plover (*Charadrius vociferus*) in these islands. His eye and ear and memory never worked together to better purpose. The Scilly Register of birds, which he had himself inaugurated, contains the following entry *s.d.* January 12, 1885:

Frequented the west end of the Long Pool, Tresco for several days. The note was very remarkable: two notes (a $\frac{1}{2}$ tone apart) of medium pitch run into one another, rather plaintive yet clamorous, repeated often while on the wing. The flight was not very rapid, but powerful. Habit on the ground like that of a Ring Plover.

To his father he wrote from Cambridge on January 18:

I had $1\frac{1}{2}$ hours with Vingoe [the Penzance naturalist] who seems quite unaltered; he is 78 in May next. I brought him *the* bird, which is, as I half expected, the *Kildeer Plover*. I shot it on Wednesday afternoon at the little pool E. of the Long Pool. Its note was a beautiful whistling cry, a sort of compound note, repeated continually as it flew; and could be heard all over the place. The *chestnut* tail coverts were the first thing I noticed (after the *note*); they shewed conspicuously as it flew, and would have been enough to identify it by, even if I had not got it. I have an impression it has occurred in England, but cannot remember where. Of course you can see it in any American Ornithology. I shall have it set up here soon, I hope, when you shall see it. It must, I think, eventually go back to Tresco, as Algy has become very keen about having birds, and has taken great trouble to have good cases to put them in. And really the great thing is to have seen it alive. Vingoe was immensely delighted with it; it is delightful to see such a real naturalist. . . . The bird was quite fat and in good condition, so it had been about these parts for some time, I suppose. The tail was a little frayed, but, as it is very long, that is not so surprising[1].

Four years later, and far from Scilly, he thought he heard the cry again, on November 3, 1889: "By Great St Mary's heard a note like the Kildeer Plover, loudly resounding. Stopped Athena Clough's cab, and they all heard it."

Cambridge from 1872 to 1923 gave him few occasions for ornithological remarks, yet he let none pass that offered. In July, 1905, he found a Great Crested Grebe swimming on the sluggish stream in front of Brookside.

Snipe were still to be heard and seen drumming over Coe Fen and always made him look up. He scrupulously noted the arrival and departure of migrants. Late in September, 1890, he writes, "Mr P— tells me of SWIFTS by hundreds perching on telegraph wires; which shews the necessity of recording only one's own observations."

The story of the Little Peewit must be told in his wife's words:

One day he came back from the Library with a tiny bird in his hand, a baby lap-wing which had been found by one of the staff just outside the Library (on the steps opposite the Senate House); how it got there remains a mystery. Of course it was brought straight to him; I think he gave it some drops

---

[1] The coloured plate in Lord Lilford's *British Birds* is from this specimen. Jenkinson noted in the Scilly bird-book (January 11, 1899) that he had identified the bird, before he shot it, by the help of the *American Ornithology* in the Library.

of water; at any rate it became quite well and lively after he brought it home (it was on a Saturday evening) and he fed it with green-fly and anything of the small grub kind we could find, and presently set it down on the lawn, where it ran about to our great delight, calling its tiny, plaintive cry. We made it a bed for the night in a small basket, and all next day we rejoiced to watch it running happily about, but alas! towards evening we thought a more substantial meal than green-fly might be beneficial, and he gave it a bit of snail; we think the sliminess of this meal must have choked it for, to our distress, it slowly shewed signs of expiring! I shall never forget watching him standing for quite an hour with this little creature in his hand in the garden, in the waning sunshine. He hoped the warmth of the sun would revive it, but at last it died, and he brought it in, and we both wept over its tiny body. I wish I could give a picture of him as he stood there with the little bird in his hand, which he seemed to be offering in appeal to the last rays of the sun[1].

This tenderness towards dumb creatures—he was a loyal member of the R.S.P.C.A. so long as it kept clear of anti-vivisection bigotry—was expressed in countless ways: clearing horses and cows of flies, saving ducks from being stoned by boys, etc. But it did not extend to rats, sparrows (their avian counterpart), marauding cats, blue-bottles, *Stomoxys*, slugs, snails, cockroaches, and other agents of mischief. Such he harried and slew without qualm or compunction: *e.g.*,

"Dowsed the yellow cat in the waterbutt."
"Annie had gathered 560 snails which I squashed."
"Coming home, killed slugs for an hour and read *Hain* till nearly 1."

[1] Cf. *Fragrance of Sweet Memories*, pp. 34 ff.

Chapter XI

PERSONAL CHARACTERISTICS

HIS ruthless treatment of baleful beasts indicated in the last chapter had its counterpart in his attitude towards human wrong-doing and stupidity. Although he was extraordinarily forgiving to the penitent and indulgent to frailty, not from acquiescence in the fault, but out of sheer pity and in hope of amendment, his moral wrath when roused was terrible to see.

One day he invited a number of little rough children into the garden to look at the flowers....While he was gathering a bunch for each, two boys had slipped away unseen into the kitchen part of the garden and were pocketing some apples; when they were missed, found, and caught, his quiet anger terrified both them and me; with white face and blazing eyes he ordered them out of the garden at once, and when I feebly faltered that I thought he had been over stern, he said, "Not at all, those boys were thieving; they've got to learn their lesson."[1]

His judgements were often severe. We have already seen some, in connexion with criticisms of Bradshaw's work by the incompetent; but there were others on his own account, *e.g.*,

Do you know by name ——, editor of the ——, which I began to take in but left off for its illiterateness? He is now Vicar of —— near here; of such are vicars made, and he came to the Library expecting special privileges! He is one of the most loathsome men I ever saw, and Rogers (who tolerates much) thinks the same. Sayle says I conducted the conversation well, and that he doesn't think he will court another. If I did, I am glad: I was quite polite.

At the Library he suffered fools without gladness:

"—— asks (for some one else) how to find an illustration of seventh century costume! Another man wants to know whether he had better settle *here* or at Oxford: so I explained the ad-

[1] Cf. *Fragrance of Sweet Memories*, p. 30.

vantages of the Bodleian." "—— came to see κειμήλια for more than an hour, without any apparent advantage to him and certainly none to me." "Was invaded by two clerics desirous of providing themselves with arguments against Agnosticism. I suggested reading the Agnostics rather than their opponents." "—— complained that the chemistry books did not all stand together. We found this meant that the *sizes* were separated, and a few feet apart. Aldis and I went with him to the shelves, but after twenty minutes we made no impression. I class him with —— who once came to complain that our copy of Luther on *Galatians* was not good enough for him. I was told afterwards that he was known to be one of the stupidest people here." "Found the Library infested by ——. Rogers fed him with historical tracts."

He was very strict with men who tried to wriggle out of paying their petty fines for books unreturned or who failed to account for irregularities: "A horrid member of the Senate attempted to get off a fine of 10s. without success." A short correspondence with such an one ends thus:

Sir, I have to acknowledge your letter of December 1, stating that it was through forgetfulness that you committed a breach of the rules on the 10th of November. It seems to me that it would have been very simple to say so at once. Your use of the word Inquisitor I do not understand.

He was not afraid of administering a public rebuke, though he did it in a way of his own which disarmed resentment. A man was fanning himself with his programme. Jenkinson leaned over and said, "Are you going to wave your programme all through the concert, Sir? For if so, I had better go home."

A learned Vandal was wetting his forefinger to turn the leaves of a book. Jenkinson silently caught his hand and laid it on the table.

It was not mere love of paradox but a dislike of pretension in any form that led to such flings as the following: "I see in the *Saturday* Tyrrell has been putting his foot into it in the matter of the French language. What can we say for a classical education if it does not teach us οὐδὲ εἰδέναι νομίζειν?" "The people who accomplish things are the people who do things badly." Or in speaking of a man of lowly origin whose actions were open to blame: "I suppose one must make allowances, so far as it is ever permitted to make allowance." Or his objection to the perpetual signature in full of three recondite and alliterative names by a man whom he did not like. When someone said, "Well, but how about Arthur James Balfour?" "Oh!" replied Jenkinson, "that's quite different." He was never a tease, but he was full of fun:

Mrs Jebb flattered me very much once by complimenting me on my perception of chaff, a faculty which she considers rare among the English. She says she is always having to explain to people things which plainly she would never have said if she had meant them. That is just my complaint.

This whimsicality, with his happy turn of phrase[1], certainly added zest to his conversation and rendered him an incomparable companion.

But the real charm of his character was his innocence. He did good actions and thought good thoughts with as little effort as he drew breath, and he never measured either by any conscious standard. Of course deep down there was the Christian training which in his later years reasserted itself. But for a long while, from his student days, he refrained from any outward expression of his religion. As a young Fellow he did not go to College Chapel, because he did not like worshipping in a crowd; but he was not at all desirous that his example should be followed by his juniors. He did not approve of the organ-loft or the ante-chapel as a substitute for the body of the building, thinking their atmosphere undevotional. He went to the village church either alone or with the family when he was away on a visit, and he noted the performance of the parson and the choir.

"Good Friday, 1914 (at Lamport): I went to church by my-

---

[1] A pair of *calembours* come into my mind and seem worth recording. *Nemo repente fuit Tirpitzimus* was a valentine of his in the *Cambridge Review* during the War, which got copied into other papers, to his surprise and pleasure.

"Too many hooks spoil the cloth," he said when his wife was fumbling with a dress. And, in a letter, "Daisy is playing Penelope with some knitting, of which the directions are obscure; and as the rows are very long, her undoing is complete."

self. Saw Mr Pitchford and spoke to the boys about rising to a higher note clean with no *portamento.*"

At Cambridge he read household prayers until domestic interruptions—the butcher and baker at the door, etc.—rendered it intolerable. His presence in college chapels was principally obtained by funeral services, of the reverent and proper rendering of which he was very jealous; but he went with alacrity to hear Dr Armitage Robinson whenever he preached, noting the text and manner of the sermon. August 13, 1914: "Sermon by the Dean of Wells—worthy of the occasion; he evidently was himself deeply moved." November 15, 1914: "The Dean of Wells preached on Ephesians v, 16, 'Redeeming the time because the days are evil.'"

No one would expect him to be a student of dogmatics. But how few, even of professed theologians, who read or hear read 1 Corinthians xv, 42 ff., apprehend the true meaning of the words, "It is sown in corruption; it is raised in incorruption." Nine out of ten understand them of committal of the body to the ground. Jenkinson instinctively felt that St Paul was speaking of birth into a corrupt world and not of burial[1]. After Bradshaw's funeral he said to me, "Ask your theological friends about it." And he always wondered why in the previous verse even the Revised Version kept "*for* one star differeth from another star," etc., instead of translating, "yea, one star," etc.

His reason revolted from Romanism and ritualism, and his taste from revivalism or Dissent. He had great sympathy with the Society of Friends and their spirituality, but yet more with the piety of George Herbert and the Carolines—though not with their ecclesiastical policy. Probably his ideal churchman and divine in modern times was Dr Hort—partly no doubt because he was Bradshaw's friend. He read the *Life and Letters* with avidity and gave or recommended the book freely to others.

He was not, as a rule, happy at a "High" service; he did not

[1] This is Calvin's interpretation, and Jenkinson certainly never read Calvin.

think that the Holy Communion Office lends itself to elaborate ceremonial and much music although he had a great affection for Merbecke's *Kyrie* and *Credo*. But his wife draws a touching picture of him at a service in Salisbury Cathedral:

We went to Salisbury in September, 1922, for my niece Katharine Stewart's confirmation, which took place on a Saturday. It was a very wonderful and beautiful occasion; he was not well, but managed to be present, and it made him very happy. Katharine and her mother and the rest of the party had to leave that day: my husband and I stayed on. Next day (Sunday) we went to the morning service in the Cathedral.... The service was beautiful, full of the peculiar and noble dignity of our English cathedral services. My dear smiled as he took my hand and hummed the hymn the choir were singing, under his breath, as we walked up to the altar and back[1].

On the other hand a funeral service in a Nonconformist chapel in 1898 he found to be

.... tiring to stand through (with George Foster and Stokes, while O.B. and such pushed through and got seats), especially the address and "prayer" (which was an address in *oratio obliqua*, with a beginning and end tacked on). These, and the final hymn sung with great energy, seemed very incongruous.

His political views were Conservative to the point of paradox if not of reaction. I heard him at a dinner party in 1886 declare that the Reform Bill of 1832 was the thin end of the wedge or the beginning of the end. Yet this was within four years of the famous contested University election of 1882 when he worked vigorously, though without result, for the return of the Liberal candidate, Professor James Stuart, "a man whom you can trust." Jenkinson was indeed a follower of Gladstone until he felt that the old statesman's idealism was carrying him into the region of the undesirable and the unattainable. He was dead against Home Rule in any form and his dislike of it stiffened as years went on. This was certainly fostered by the journals he preferred to read—the *Morning Post* (in spite of its "howlers")

[1] *Fragrance of Sweet Memories*, p. 44.

and Mr Leo Maxse's organ. "I read *The National Review* here, which if rather violent gives me great satisfaction; though I am not enough in the middle of things to know what he means." (April 21, 1912.)

Demagogues were his abhorrence; one conspicuous politician he dismissed as a "mendacious little blackguard"; but he kept familiar relations with certain Liberal leaders his old friends, and we have seen that he was attracted by Mr John Burns at a chance meeting (*vide supra*, p. 70). His vote of recent years was consistently given on principle for the constitutional party. Thus at the election in January, 1910, he writes, "I expect that here as in so many cases the Radical is the better man. But in the present position of things that is of no importance, unless he is good enough to direct the Cabinet."

In Academic matters he was generally opposed to what he considered unnecessary change, though he was by no means a habitual *non-placet*. He was against the abolition of compulsory Greek in the Little-Go and, while eager for the education of women, he resisted their admission to government of the University, which he regarded as men's business; and on each division he found himself ranged against his best friends. Except on topics which touched his own studies and occupations, or raised a special point of principle, he took little part in public discussions; and when he did, it was not with much apparent effect, for he was no orator. But his fly-sheets shew that he was a cogent advocate on paper, and as has been well said "he was one of those men who when they declare themselves can turn a battle."[1]

Jenkinson was no adept in modern literature; book catalogues and the daily paper, both for its news and its jargon, supplied a momentary diversion before and after, and often during meals, and he had not the habit of reading in bed. But he enjoyed listening while he pinned his flies, leaving the choice to his wife—it was generally Miss Thackeray, or Jane Austen, or Charles

[1] Cf. an appreciation by Sir Geoffrey Butler in *The Library Association Record* for December, 1923.

Dickens. He was moved to tears by passages of special beauty in the Bible or Shakespeare or Christina Rossetti, and to undisguised anger by lapses from good taste. He had his favourite writers and his *bêtes noires*. He cherished Tennyson chiefly for the sake of his son Hallam, Keats and Herrick and the Elizabethan Song-writers for their music, Browning for his thought, and Robert Bridges, among later poets, for both[1]. But he was not a worshipper at any shrine, nor an adventurer into the unknown, nor a prey to the fascination of detective stories, and his moral sense revolted against the reckless handling of sex-problems by novelists. Hawthorne's *Scarlet Letter* was one of the few works of fiction in which he found a tolerable treatment of a delicate theme. What he disliked in Thomas Hardy was not so much his pessimism as his pursuit of the unusual and the unsavoury; situations in which he was not likely to find himself did not interest him, and he would have subscribed to the generalization of Boileau, whom he probably never read, that the only legitimate object of poetic imitation is the universal and the permanent, not freaks of nature or monstrous phenomena.

This classical bias appears in his admiration for Fielding. Thus to his sister in 1885:

Have you ever read Fielding's *Amelia*? I had no notion how good it was, until I began the other day to read it again. It is genius without waywardness, and might be a good model to some of our geniuses of today who think they must kick over the traces to assert their superiority. One sentence is too delightful not to quote. Speaking of the sight of Amelia and her children, when her husband has been locked up, he says, "These... tragical sights...afford a juster motive to tears and grief in the beholder than it would be *to see all the heroes who have ever infested the earth, hanged all together in a string.*"

George Meredith exercised on Jenkinson alternate repulsion and attraction. His manner "often perverse and pedantic" reminded him of Wagner, and his personages, though living, seemed too far removed from the ordinary. So he remarks

[1] He followed Mr Bridges's metrical experiments with great interest and approval especially as expounded to him orally by their maker.

"Sayle lent me *The Egoist* yesterday to beguile the time. Of course I wasted much of my day over it. It is wonderful stuff, interesting but sometimes exasperating: and most of the time one stops to wonder how any one could invent such queer stuff. That can hardly be the best kind of art." "The only person I know who converses like any of his characters is Lord Acton [he might have added Meredith himself]; he has just that way of picking up the last speaker." But he could read *Diana* "all day" on holiday, finishing it at 3.30 a.m., and of another number of the great comedy he writes to his sister, "I am glad you found *The Amazing Marriage* so interesting. It is an amazing book! One is repelled, but more often attracted than repelled; and carried along irresistibly by the stream. His characters are so alive, and however improbable one accepts them without misgiving. I do not think that is always so— *e.g.* in *The Egoist*."

He adored Scott, "probably the greatest creator since Shakespeare," but he did not care much for R. L. Stevenson, maintaining, against Verrall, that his humour was forced (except perhaps in *Catriona*) and his style artificial. He was easily put off by faulty observation of nature, unsound logic, and obscurity. Sometimes he records his sentiments in his Diary:

"Quiller-Couch hates R. Jefferies as much as I do."
"Read *Far From the Madding Crowd* through and enjoyed some touches of it very much; but the coincidences do not seem natural and some of the sentences are portentously clumsy; and occasionally the author seems to forget who is speaking."
"Read some of the end of *Robert Elsmere*, and did not feel tempted to read the rest."

He cordially disliked *The Epic of Hades*, and his irritation at *The Natural Law and the Spiritual Life* found expression in fierce marginal annotations. He was impatient of offences against pure English in speech or writing, and of modern printers' deviations from old-established custom.

I suppose there is nothing to be done; but I confess dear ——'s letter, *full* of slang, made my heart sink. Can you not urge her to write like an educated person? I am glad the young ones are not so bad.

He very much disliked the dropping of the second s in the genitive of a noun ending in s: James's, Thomas's, etc., and even more so, and with better reason perhaps, the habit of dividing English words at the consonant.

He urges Duff, in 1905, to stand out against it:

> I hope you will not let the printers (if they wish to) perpetrate such word-divisions as 'defin-itely,' 'typograph-ically,' 'confirm-ing,' 'diction-ary,' 'import-ant,' 'liturgic-ally,' 'natural-ized'— for they make me very uncomfortable; and spring from a pedantry which as usual is contrary to practical reason. Why they must change the old practice I do not know. The rule has to be used by the compositor, and should therefore be one that he can understand, *not* etymological. Besides this is just one of those things where change is bad in itself, because one does not even notice the divisions one is accustomed to, while new inventions bring one up sharp.

He sedulously collected solecisms and grammatical blunders in the columns of the daily press in the interests of the Pure English Society, though I do not know that they ever found their way to headquarters. The S. P. E. Tracts were carefully studied. Witness the following letter to R. Bridges (Oct. 6, 1922):

> I have read Fowler's Treatise on Grammatical Inversion with great interest. It introduces method into what have been hitherto chaotic patches of dissatisfaction in my mind. He gives (on page 10 and pages 15 and 16) two instances of inversion after "than": but merely treats it among "Relatives and Compara-tives." What he says on p. 16 is, I think, quite true: "If the verb is omitted, no harm is done"—that is to say, the verb is thrown back where it is not important enough to come at the end. These instances after "than" are among the commonest (I know I have some bad ones somewhere, if I did not give them to Jackson). I have just found one as long ago as 1865 in W. G. Palgrave's *Narrative of a Year's Journey*, vol. I, p. 180: "Who is supposed to be better acquainted with letters than *are* the average of his countrymen." Here it seems to me

not only that the "are" might be omitted, but that it would be omitted*.

> * I think I mean that the "is supposed to be" covers the whole sentence, and the "are" spoils the sense of that.

A year or two ago I noticed Dicey writing something like this: " . . . . than *was* Napoleon." I wrote and asked him about it: at first he did not understand my point—then he said that no doubt he might have left out the "was." But he seemed quite unconscious that it was not the natural thing to write.

Such passages are of interest, although the points they raise may seem trivial, because Jenkinson wrote so little for the press. He was indeed singularly loath to do so in spite of his uncommon gift of terse, strong, and picturesque expression. He confessed his own incapacity for a work of *de longue haleine* when he criticized one of Duff's books in 1894: "I think you have something to learn in respect of style here and there; and as you know I can't write ten consecutive lines myself, I am not afraid of saying so." He certainly did not like writing, and, although not afraid of controversy, he seldom screwed himself up to the point of a letter to the newspapers. When he did, it was effective. He took so much pains about everything to which he set his hand that he resented the editor's inevitable blue pencil, whether in the obituary article of his old friend A. B. Farm for which he made elaborate preparation, or in the note on Hicks of Bodmin which he despatched from his hospital-bed to *The Sunday Times*.

It is somewhat surprising that being the son of his father and himself so observant, so sensitive to form and colour, he should never have plied brush or pencil. An occasional rough sketch in a letter suggests that he could have drawn if he had liked or taken lessons. As it is, if he succeeded in representing an object it was by sheer force of intellect and not by acquired skill. His admiration of good draughtsmanship from the Anglo-Saxon MSS. in Corpus Library to the current number of *Punch* was unbounded, and there are many who owe their first plunge into

126

the magic of Turner to a visit under Jenkinson's guidance to the water-colours in the Fitzwilliam Museum.

I take at haphazard from his correspondence an example of descriptive writing. It is of a friend's house near Oxford:

He has thrown out such wings and bows that I hardly know where I am; but the hall is a magnificent sort of basilica, transverse, with columns, Cretan in character—a Minotaur, etc. on the pavement. The drawing-room with three windows to S.W. and a vista down a path between rising trees, conifers, etc. Another vista more to the left commands a lake, with an island, made by damming up a stream in a ravine. In the foreground are sheets of winter-flowering heath. We look across miles of low country to higher ground in the distance, and tonight over that there is a hard, crinkled bank of dark clouds like a range of mountains: and over that there *was* a sunset, very restricted, but as brilliant as a handful of jewels. Now only Venus, not less brilliant.

He who can write like that has little need to paint.

Like Pascal before his conversion, Jenkinson loved to have everything about him of the best, though unlike the great ascetic he never blamed himself for his fastidiousness. He rejoiced not only in good joinery, good binding, good paper, but also in good wine and good cooking. It is to him alone that the Trinity kitchens owe a dish for which they have long been famous—"Crème brûlée." This he had tasted when an undergraduate in a Scotch house. He offered the recipe to the college cook, who declined it. When he became a Fellow he imposed it, to the lasting benefit of all concerned. Again, "A boiled apple-dumpling, apple broken up and *decored*, a sort of miniature apple-pudding, perfectly lovely," served to him at a London restaurant in 1915, is celebrated in Diary and letter. He was sometimes less fortunate. We read of "a worm an inch and a half long in my minced beef—I had to have champagne"; and of a cockroach in his cake, the apology of the baker being that she always strained the water!

His interest in books and journals was sensibly affected by the *Ausstattung*. He dropped one meritorious periodical because of the baseness of the paper on which it was printed and was heartily censured therefor by Mr David Nutt.

For fear of legal action I withhold the name of the Diary which he used with reluctance for twenty-four years and at length abandoned, writing on December 31, 1917, "And so I part company with ——, vulgar outside and stupid inside: criticism produced no satisfaction."

An empty copy of Smith's Official Octavo Diary (for 1884) which had belonged to Bradshaw contains some retrospective entries by Jenkinson who found it when clearing up; in 1918 he adopted this *format* again and used it to the end.

He rarely found a pen that really pleased him though he tried all sorts from an etching nib to a goose-quill. So his hand-writing varied. It is not true that script is always the reflection of the mind. Dean Stanley and Dr Westcott alone refute such a generalization, to say nothing of medieval scribes, whose in-telligence seems often in inverse ratio to their calligraphy. But no one who ever received a letter from Jenkinson can have doubted for a moment that it came from a scholar. It was not until he fell under Bradley's influence at Marlborough that he began to take trouble with his pen; and after Bradley, Bradshaw, whom he copied whether consciously or not. The final result was as fine an example as can be desired of flowing cursive, legible, rapid, and beautiful in line. I think it worth while to reproduce in facsimile these changes of style.

He was eminently and heartily sociable, delighting in the company of his fellow-men, in nearly all of whom he found something to like, and able to derive pleasure from the most dreary function and the stiffest luncheon or dinner. Always content with the entertainment which his town and University provided, he greatly resented attempts, in the 'eighties, to Londonize Cambridge by what are now called "week-end" parties. He seldom visited the fashionable world. Once he was taken by Dr Norman Moore to a Conversazione at the Royal Academy, which he described as "a wilderness of human beings, among whom horrors were most conspicuous. I identified the

Dear Nelly,

I have no time for a letter yet—

I have no recollection of paying for blankets, so surely did it—

Penlech is what I used once or twice as my own authority for skins; it must at least be fair. It is the best thing I know of. I have my Russ: dictionary. I have just got a German book a Phillips, nearly 800 pages ..... 8vo !! — De Greco, grand... blotlam your marine!

....didn't he inquire about the Crane; I was never so tired out by an ... before. I am glad Huntsman was so pleasant. Bülow played the 1st 2 movements of no.14 very well; the allegretto slow. But when he came to the Presto, the start was ... too fast, too piano, & he didn't get to the woolly ... with anything like precision. Then there was an exaggeration & abundance of sf & fp all through which disgusted me: I had much rather not have heard it—

FACSIMILE OF LETTER (reduced about one-third) TO HIS SISTER IN 1876

Turner & I dine at 4.30 this time, which gets digestion over in time for a good evenings work. Turner has got the page in his year for reading the lessons in Chapel, so his honours are mounting up. He has got 3 pupils in Pol. Economy + is quite happy: We had, as well as Chopin, Schumann P.M. for Sterndale Bennett. Trio begins

you will guess the pace. Goodnight. Love to all + M.A. Yr. loving

The Bach was thumped cruelly: Mendelssohn all very good indeed: & do Chopin, who however, used all new terms. Liszt struck me as a brutal wonderful time — + the whole quite stupefying.

Tell me exactly what the publication is which has won for me. Last night at 12 o'clock just as I was coming away for Pypets trap toddled in walked Turner, + trays toddled in walked Turner, + we sat there reading Shakespeare etc for 6½ hours: when I went to bed, but they did not. We all agreed that it was worth doing as in a way, + I feel none the worse.

Southread
Chaucer Road
Cambridge
1907 Oct. 28

My dear Duff,

It seems difficult to be-
lieve that twenty years ago
we were unknown to each
other. At any rate I am glad
it has been so long, for from
the first you have been a great
help to me, from the time when
I was editing Bradshaw, +
knew no one to whom an
early printed book meant anything, continuously till now,
when the times have sprung
up, and I have almost forgotten the little I ever knew, and
am consequently rejoiced to be
given an occasional glimpse
into the higher regions of bibliography. I was delighted with
your paper on Scottish armorial
bindings, and astonished that
you had got together so much
material. [This side of the paper
won't take the ink - + that
always puts me off.]

At the Vatican, besides Ehrle,
I only knew H. M. Bannis-
ter, who has devoted much time
to collating Hispanica for me.
If you let me know what

FACSIMILE OF LETTER (*reduced about one-third*) TO E. G. DUFF IN 1907 lost enough absurdity. The weather is not very helpful. While my father and sister were here, we had equatorial gales (malgrant): & now we have dull sundass & frosty calms, & everyone has colds & chills.

My wife sends kind remembrance.

I have rashly undertaken to give the Sandars lectures next year, sure of them! I wish myself well through it; but—how—?

your affectionate friend
F. Jenkinson

(even when I do not sign my-self so.)

you want, I would ask him; & if it is not his sent-friend, he would probably suggest someone else, i?

Here is my one,

I am glad to hear of your volume of Handlists. They are very useful. We have had a sad autumn.

At the end of August my brother was taken ill, and after a month of increasing drowsiness, he died on Sept. 27. It proved to be an abscess in the brain for which nothing could have been done. The cause is unknown. It has cut short a very useful and happy life.

M³s Balfour, Maitland, Michael Foster, and Newton were a heavy

Rev. H. R. Haweis." He was a member of the Savile for a short time, but resigned in 1892, and joined no other London Club. College Feasts and meetings of the two dining-clubs to which he belonged, the Society, a purely local, and the *Ad Eundem*, an Oxford and Cambridge affair, were a constant snare, and generally resulted in a headache and a day in bed. His digestion was very delicate, and excited by friendship and good talk he ate at random; above all, the inevitable accompaniment of tobacco-smoke poisoned him. He once, in 1890, smoked a cigar in Pembroke Combination Room and recorded it as an event (I note that he lost a cigar-case in 1881); but he had no taste for tobacco, and he waxed eloquent against the cigarette habit in men, women, and especially boys. Although exceedingly temperate in his use of wine he was a good judge of vintages; and when Tennyson stayed with him in college in 1886 and asked leave to mix water with his port (like Boswell's Lord Erroll), Jenkinson was almost as much shocked as W. Aldis Wright, who had fetched the precious bottle from the cellar. This visit is mentioned in Lord Tennyson's *Memoir*, vol. II, p. 326. Jenkinson's own account of it is as follows:

1886, August 7. Hallam turned up from Cromer with his wife and father. We made him sit in the garden till tea, then took him in a boat on the Backs till dinner. He seemed to like the idea of being in college once more, so we put him upstairs in Glaisher's room[1]. Wright produced some of the '34 port (which he was allowed to mix with water, to his great joy) and Madeira. I had a long talk with Mrs T. while the others smoked downstairs.

It is difficult to say in what society he was at his best, for the level seldom dropped, but perhaps it was with children of all ages. He loved them from their babyhood and the strictest nurse and the most anxious mother could confide the bundle of long clothes to his arms without a qualm. He had wise counsel

---

[1] *I.e.* above Jenkinson's rooms looking down "that long walk of limes." The horse-chestnut which stands in the middle of the Court was planted at his suggestion in 1885. "It will look enlarging, and stop view and noise, when it grows."

to offer on the management of infants, while his treatment of the child as it grew, carefully adapted to its ripening intelligence, was a lesson in education. He was never pedantic or boring or impatient, for with all his impulsiveness he had complete control over his own moods; yet he never suffered naughtiness or clumsiness to go unreproved. He watched them progress and recorded it in his book. He taught them, and their elders, how to handle books and flowers. "Remember you should always treat a book like glass," he said to a young library assistant. He had always something interesting or beautiful to shew them. His letters to his small nephews and nieces are models of what letters to children should be, and he delighted in their painful scrawls in reply.

Thus to his niece, aged four (a beautiful example of *minuscule* with a sketch of the bat):

1907, September 19.

My dear Jean,

I wish you had been here to take care of Auntie Daisy when the bat came in, late one night. She was reading to me a book called "The Beloved Vagabond," when suddenly she stopped, gave a little scream, and was at the door in a moment! I looked up from my microscope, and saw a large black thing moving so quickly that the room seemed to be full of it. I went downstairs and got my net; and very soon caught it; it was the largest fly my net had ever had in it. I saw it was one of the bats with very long ears, much longer than a donkey's: for when it lays them down, they reach quite half-way down its back. When it puts them up, they must be able to catch the tiniest sound. Next morning when I had looked at it, I thought Jean's house [the old greenhouse] would be a nice quiet place for it to sleep in: for you know when the day comes, all the bats hang themselves up by their hind legs and so sleep till the evening. But this bat did not want to sleep there: and it spread its wings, and flew past the greenhouse and round towards the house, and then—it went straight in at the south-east side window of the Fly Room, by which it had come in the night before. I never saw it again, but when it went, having no visiting cards, it left on my table the hind wing of a fat moth which it had eaten as an entrée before it went to look for the rest of its dinner outside.

1907 September 15

SOUTHMEAD,

[2 enclosures.]

CHAUCER ROAD,

CAMBRIDGE.

My dear Jean,

I wish you had been here to take care of Auntie Daisy when the bat came in, late one night.

She was reading to me a book called 'The Beloved Vagabond' when suddenly she stopped, gave a little scream, and was at the door in a moment.' I looked up from my microscope, and saw a large black thing moving about so quickly that the room seemed to be full of it.

I went downstairs and got my net;

and very soon caught it; it was the largest fly my net had ever had in it. I saw it was one of the bats with very long ears, much longer than a donkey's ears: for when it lays them down, they reach quite halfway down its back. When it puts them up, they must be able to catch the tiniest sound.

Next morning when I had looked at it, I thought Jean's house would be a nice quiet place for it to sleep in: for you know when the day comes all the bats hang them themselves up by their hind legs and so sleep till the evening.

But this bat did not want to sleep there: and it spread its

wings, and flew past the greenhouse, and round towards the house, and then — it went straight in at the south-east side window of the Fly Room, by which it had come in the night before. I never saw it again, but when it went, having no visiting cards, it left on my table the hind wing of a fat moth which it had eaten as an entrée before it went to look for the rest of its dinner outside.

Do you remember Annie's little girl Lily? She came to see us on Tuesday with her mummy, and she said she liked Jean's house better than Auntie Daisy's. But as there was no one here to play with her,

Lander came and carried her through the
hedge to play with his little girl in the
garden next door: and they became
great friends, and talked to each other,
and played till dinner time; and then
good Mister Lander carried her back.

The rockery has several kinds
of beautiful butterflies feasting
on the flowers that grow in it:
and there are frogs that live under
the stones; and one day Auntie
Daisy heard one croaking!

Today all the peas that were left were
picked, to be sown next year! and we
collected all the straw and made a
great bonfire by the light of the moon:
and now it is bed-time, and I expect
it is still burning. Good night: love and
kisses from A.D. and your affectionate Uncle Mig.

Do you remember Annie's little girl Lily? She came to see us on Tuesday with her mummy, and she said she liked Jean's house better than Auntie Daisy's. But as there was no one to play with her, Lander [the gardener] came and carried her through the hedge to play with his little girl in the garden next door: and they became great friends, and talked to each other and played till dinner time, and then good Mister Lander carried her back. The rockery has several kinds of beautiful butterflies feasting on the flowers that grow in it: and there are frogs that live under the stones; and one day Auntie Daisy heard one croaking! Today all the peas that were left were picked, to be sown next year: and we collected all the straw and made a great bonfire by the light of the moon: and now it is bed-time, and I expect it is still burning. Good night: love and kisses from A. D. and your affectionate Uncle Mig.

Consequently they all adored him. They saw in him something like the Figure which they were taught to venerate above all others. "I think Uncle Mig is like Jesus," said one. *Ex ore infantium.*

Nor was his affection confined to his own kith and kin and the small people of his friends. He tried to teach the urchins whom he encountered on his daily walk across Coe Fen what to do and what not to do towards beasts and birds and plants. One of his last actions in Cambridge was to bestow some cakes of his particular "Sapon" soap to soothe a ragamuffin's itching skin. They knew him and greeted him as he passed; once with, "We've seen your picture in the Museum," having wandered into the Fitzwilliam during play-time.

Something of his outward appearance may be gathered from Sargent's masterpiece and the snapshots reproduced in this book; and indeed black and white is not a bad medium for the portrayal of a face from which all colour was absent. It was like parchment, lined and wrinkled, often drawn with pain and fatigue, but even in moments of acute suffering liable to be lit with a smile of peculiar radiance which cheated you into acquiescence with his asseveration, "There's not much amiss with me." His Diary and his letters tell another tale, registering an incredible number of bad nights and blank days, and confessing great weariness and distress. He observed his own state of health with curiosity, taking his temperature twice daily (normally 97·6 in the morning and 96·6 at night) and entering it in his diary together with readings of the outside thermometer and the direction of the wind which he occasionally qualified with suitable comments, "N.E. accursed," "E. infernal."

My plans are quite upset by a collapse of the confounded machine to which I am attached...

It's funny, I don't seem able to keep quite well for more than a week on end...

I spent the day miserably in bed with one of the usual attacks; post-nasal catarrh *ad nauseam* and continually bad headache most of the night.

Such a remark as "Today I felt really well and capable all day" is unfortunately very rare.

That he should have accomplished as much as he did, and have kept so bright to the end is evidence of a singular victory of soul over matter.

He was exceedingly spare, nay, almost emaciated, but when not prostrated by headache his movements were brisk and lively. His walk was an easy swing, loose at the knees, the feet kept straight, leisurely unless he had to catch a train or overtake a friend, and then he would run with short steps at a surprising pace. I remember coming back with him late one night from a meeting of the Greek Play Committee at Scroope House. He insisted on dancing all down Trumpington Street, two steps on one foot, then two on the other, to get the stiffness out of his joints.

His voice was not exactly musical, but singularly pleasant, rapid and gentle, of medium pitch; his language, never pedantic, was free from every sort of offence against good taste.

Though not in the least a dandy he was fastidious about the cut and fit of his clothes, which once donned he wore to extreme antiquity. His hats were a regiment of veterans and he did not always remember to choose the youngest when he went out. His usual habit was a suit of black, but on holiday he broke out into Harris tweeds and a bright coloured tie. He was very

AT CAMBRIDGE   1910

sensitive about his hair and hated from a schoolboy to have it ruffled or wetted by rain. He records his first experience of an alien razor, Dec. 28, 1894: "Had my hair cut at Hill's and was *shaved* for the first time in my life: more *pressure* than I expected: drew blood in several places."

Seventy years are a long life; thirty-four years a long tenure of office; and Jenkinson had reached and passed the term which Royal Commissioners assign to servants of the University. Yet no one, I imagine, thought him too old for his position, nor did he feel himself superannuated. He was one with whom Time stood still. On his sixty-ninth birthday he drove back from a friend's house through the streets of Cambridge wearing his grey hat wreathed with roses and lavender: a token of his triumph over the scythe-bearer. He looked forward to the operation which proved fatal as a means of recovering strength for further work in the Library, and after that to a quiet corner in the building where he could continue his pet studies after he had surrendered the keys. And it may be said here that to no one would he have surrendered them more willingly than to him who now sits in his place. His last letters written just before and in the midst of his hospital experience, which it is difficult to read today without emotion, all tell the same tale of hope and confidence. To E. G. Duff he wrote on July 28, 1923.

I don't often have anything interesting to report to you: but you will be interested to hear that we have just added to our collection (by the liberality of J. Charrington) a good copy of the 1473 Alost edition of the *De duobus amantibus*. We now have 3 examples of that press. I do not know whether there are any others in England. What have *you* been doing? Scholfield, who is beside me, joins in wishing you could find some excuse to visit us again. Is there any chance of it? *Not immediately*, for tomorrow I go to the hospital at Holloway for a small operation, and I do not suppose I shall be back here till some time in October. We had a visit from Pollard this week, and he found time to come twice to the Library and to take an interest in what I could shew him. He says our collection of incunabula for its size is exceptionally full of interesting things, which was pleasant to hear. He is inclined to print my systematic list of fifteenth [cent.] books in G. Dunn's library; which I should be glad of as a memorial of Dunn, but surely not many people would care for it. Sayle is getting on with his bindings, and I fancy writes to you rather oftener than I do.

To Mr A. T. Bartholomew of the University Library he wrote on August 31 as follows:

The Nook, Holford Road, Hampstead, N.W. 3.

My dear Bartholomew,

I have not much to say except to thank you for your excellent letter, which made me feel less completely an exile, and to wish you a good and beneficial holiday. The nearest places I know to your sun-bath in the Rhone Valley are Chandolin perched above Sion, and the Hotel Weisshorn, above St Luc: where I basked in the sun 30 years ago, and studied the habits and *noises* of the different kinds of grasshopper with Poulton and Burdon-Sanderson[1]; a time I always look back to with great satisfaction.

The proposal about protecting the catalogue seems a good one, *if adequate*: I suppose Zz disappears[2]. I am still rather anxious about the despatch of books to the Hague[3]. I have asked Thomas if there was no formal application from the Librarian at the Hague. I must write an explanation, to make sure of his not being offended at the informality. Horrox was an admirable courier: I should like to have seen him deliver them to the Secretary of State for Foreign Affairs himself. I am so very sorry for the poor dear Peterhouse people. Do convey my sympathy, if you see him[4].

My wife is coming up to Cambridge on Thursday for one night. But you will be starting next morning. (Private. I hope Aston told Pye of Sargent's regret that he could no longer paint portraits, but occupied himself with *less exacting work*. A very nice letter—tell Pye, if you see him[5].) Your Lavender

[1] Cf. Professor Poulton's paper on "Courtship of Certain European Acridiidae" (*Transactions of the Entom. Society* for 1896, pp. 233–252) which contains the record of observations made by him, F. V. Dickins and Jenkinson in August and September, 1895, many of them in Jenkinson's own words.

[2] Viz. by a fire-proof case which would have swallowed up the shelves lettered Zz.

[3] *Vide supra*, p. 41.

[4] The reference is to general ill-health at Peterhouse Lodge.

[5] A movement was on foot to procure a portrait of the Master of Trinity, and Mr D. Pye of Trinity was acting as secretary for the purpose.

Water has been a great comfort. Two kinds of "Old English Lavender Water"—one marked "Mitcham"—had been got for me, and both seemed *hot* and sophisticated. Yours seems cooler: and I use it often. And such a pretty bottle! I want to send this off today; and I am (for once) having a visitor, a sister-in-law, to tea—so I cannot remember whether I had anything else particularly to say to you.

Your Butler work must mean a good deal of time. If you write to F(esting) J(ones) greet him from me, and *Ord* who kindly sent me a card from Rapallo.

My wife is not in yet from shopping, or would certainly reciprocate your kind remembrance.

Yours very sincerely,

F. JENKINSON.

To Mr Cuthbertson, Secretary to the Library, he wrote under the same date: "It will not be of much use to write to me for the next week or so: after that I shall, I hope, begin to be able to take an interest in things."

To Miss Crum of Longworth Manor, whither his wife was going for rest and comfort, he says on September 2:

I can't tell you how grateful I am to you for taking care of Daisy during what to her is a *crisis*! (I look at it rather differently. A short oblivion—not so long as I already went through on July 31 without inconvenience, and then perhaps some discomfort, *but* deliverance from my tormentor.) I go into Hospital[1] on Wednesday, September 5: operation probably on Thursday morning.... We hope now that I may be able to come back here in a fortnight or so, and pick up more quickly than I could down in the Hospital: where the surroundings are somewhat depressing and deficient in repose, to put it mildly. *This* is the most exhilarating place imaginable. I see the whole of London, E. and S.E., with every varying atmosphere and sun and shadow. Soon after 6 (really 5) the sun rises level with my window and shines on my bed: I have hardly ever had that sensation before. Earlier in the night those two stars ⁂ one knows so well (are they Castor and Pollux?) look straight in on me. I have begun to do some weeding in the garden, which Miss Fullerton much appreciates. There are two wonderful collections of

[1] From his nursing home at Hampstead, where he was recuperating after the preliminary examination.

flowers from Southmead (brought by Daisy), including Porter's[1] handsome red and black geranium, and the rose-coloured malvaceous plant (? Sphaeralcia) *Convolvulus mauretanicus*. The buds go on coming out in water. Now I must finish my letter to Marganinni[2]. Love to all the family.

In a letter of the same date to Dr R. St J. Parry, Vice-Master of Trinity, answering a letter of September 5 he says:

I am gaining strength every day, I think, especially every *sunny* day. Today I did half an hour's weeding in the garden, and then lay in the hot sun, and feel all the better; but I can't walk much. Kenneth Walker will come and see me again here, and decide when I am fit to have the operation. I don't know whether that will pull me down as much as the previous treatment. I rather hope *not*, but the healing is a tedious business, and will take some time: and that will be down in Holloway and not up in this paradise. (At the same time I am grateful to everyone in Holloway, and to the whole management: and I am very sorry that their work is crippled by want of funds, 70 beds closed and much needed in that district[3].)

The operation was successful but his strength could not stand the shock. He was taken back to the Nursing Home which had become so dear to him, and there, on the morning of September 21, he breathed his last. What was mortal of him was left in Trumpington cemetery on September 25 after a funeral service of a simplicity and dignity such as he would have approved. Trinity chapel was filled from end to end (though term had not begun) with mourners, not merely come to pay formal respect but moved by a real emotion at the departure of one whose presence was a delight and a benediction.

The memory of such a character belies the philosopher and the poets who declare that the recollection of former happiness is the crown of sorrows. It is rather a consolation for the mean and ugly things of life which vex us and which dared not raise their head while he was in our midst.

[1] The Longworth gardener.   [2] His youngest niece.
[3] This is how he tried to express his practical sympathy. He wrote from his bed a letter to the *Sunday Times* correcting a quotation from *Hicks of Bodmin* (a book to which he was greatly devoted) and dated it from the Hospital. When he was asked why he had not used his Cambridge address, he said, "I thought it might do the Hospital some good if I wrote from here."

APPENDIX I

Writings

§ I. BIBLIOGRAPHY AND LIBRARY AFFAIRS.

1883 *On the Shop Sign of J. Secker.* "The Antiquary," vol. VIII, p. 86.

1886 *H. Bradshaw's List of Psalters, etc. Hymns. Note on "Sizes."* (Controlled by F. J.) Cambridge "Sarum Breviary," fasc. iii, pp. lxxxi f., cii, cxxi. (Cambridge University Press.)

1886 *H. Bradshaw's Note on Books printed by J. Siberch.* (Ed. F. J.) Bullock's "Oratio" in facsimile. (Macmillan and Bowes.)

1886 *H. Bradshaw's Note on the "Hermathena."* (Ed. F. J.) "Papyrii Gemini Hermathena" in facsimile. (Macmillan and Bowes.)

1886 *Footnotes to R. Bowes on the University Printers.* Camb. Antiq. Soc. "Communications," no. XXVI (vol. V, no. 4).

1887 *On Bookbinding.* (*Correcting Andrew Lang.*) "The Athenaeum," February 26.

1888 *On "Sizes."* (*Correcting Dr B. Richardson.*) "The Athenaeum," November 10 and 24.

1889 *Collected Papers of Henry Bradshaw.* (Ed. F. J.) (Cambridge University Press.)

1889 *On a MS. Copy of the Scala of Joh. Climacus.* Camb. Antiq. Soc. "Communications," vol. VII, p. 17.

1889 *On a Book Printed by J. Siberch.* Camb. Antiq. Soc. "Communications," vol. VII, pp. 104–105.

1890 *On a Letter from P. Kaetz to J. Siberch.* Camb. Antiq. Soc. "Communications," vol. VII, pp. 186–189.

1893 *"The Hibernensis": Two Unfinished Papers by Henry Bradshaw.* (Ed. F. J.) (Cambridge University Press.)

1898 *The First Paris Press, by H. Claudin.* (Ed. F. J. for the Bibliographical Society, *v.s.* p. 89.)

1901 *Two Fly-sheets on the Eastern Quadrangle Question.* Nov. 20 and 22.

1903 *Remarks on Rotheram's Books.* Camb. Antiq. Soc. "Communications," vol. x, p. 425.

1905 *Appeal in behalf of the Library* (in collaboration with J. W. Clark).

1905 *Address Delivered at the Opening of the Twenty-eighth Annual Meeting of the Library Association.* (Macmillan and Bowes.)

1907 *Note on a Volume from the Library of the Dominicans of Dundee.* Edinburgh Bibliographical Society.

1907 *Letter on Library Administration.* (*Answering Mr H. G. Fordham.*) "The Morning Post," Feb. 19.

1908 *Sandars Lecture on Ulric Zell.* (Not yet printed, but *vide supra*, p. 68.)

1911 *The Cambridge Memorandum* (except par. III).

1911 *Letter on the Copyright Bill.* (*Answering Mr John Murray.*) "The Times," Nov. 22.

1911 *Letter on "A Bookworm's Perplexity."*[1] "The Athenaeum," May 6.

1923 *A List of the Incunabula Collected by George Dunn.* Supplement to the Bibliographical Society's "Transactions," no. 3.

§ II. NUMISMATICS.

1883 *On a hoard of Roman Coins found at Willingham.* Camb. Antiq. Soc. "Communications," vol. v, pp. 225–231.

1886 *"Tyery's Proposals for an Irish Coinage."* (Ed. G. O. White Cooper and F. Jenkinson.) Camb. Antiq. Soc., Octavo Publications, no. XXII.

§ III. CLASSICAL.

1899 *Eight Translations into Latin, one into Greek.* Archer-Hind and Hicks's "Cambridge Compositions." (Camb. Univ. Press.)

1908 *"The Hisperica Famina," ed. with Short Introduction and Index Verborum.* (Camb. Univ. Press.)

§ IV. SCIENTIFIC.

1871 *On the Scilly Islands.* Report of the Marlborough N. H. S.

1872 *On Shells.* Report of the Marlborough N. H. S.

The following items all appeared in the "Entomologist's Monthly Magazine." Those marked * are full-dress papers; the rest are notes.

1878 *Record of Captures at Scilly in 1877, communicated by Stainton.* Vol. xv, p. 88.

1886 *On* Sphinx convolvuli *at Scilly.* Vol. xxII, p. 261.

1896 *On* Tinea vinculella. Vol. xxxII, p. 214.

1899 *On* Pyrameis cardui *at Scilly.* Vol. xxxv, p. 91.

1900 *On* Lepidoptera *at Lowestoft.* Vol. xxxvi, p. 188.

1901 (a) *On* Volucella zonaria *on a Channel Boat.*
    (b) *On* Syrphidae *at Cambridge.*
    (c) *On* Pachygaster leachii *at Cambridge.*
    (d) *On the gender of the term* Pachygaster.

---

[1] Dr A. Jessopp found himself, or rather Jenkinson found him, in possession of a little seventeenth-century book (lawfully acquired) which once belonged to the U. L. C. and bore its stamp. What were the ethics of the situation? Having aired his perplexity in *The Athenaeum* (April 15, 1911) Dr Jessopp willingly restored the volume.

(e) *On* Idia lunata *at Cambridge.*
(f) *On* Trigonometopus frontalis *near Newbury.*
(g) *On* Acletoxenus syrphoides *Frauenfeld at Cambridge.* Vol. xxxvii, pp. 299, 300.

1902 *Coloured Plate of* Acletoxenus syrphoides *Frauenfeld, illustrating Paper by Collins (presented by F. J.).* Vol. xxxviii, p. 2.
On Acletoxenus formosus *at Cambridge.* Vol. xxxviii, p. 285.

1903 *On* Platypezidae *at Cambridge.* Vol. xxxix, p. 173.
*On Verrallia aucta *and its Host.* Vol. xxxix, pp. 222–223.

(a) *On* Neopachygaster orbitalis, *Whlbg., and* Nephrocerus flavicornis, *Zett., in the New Forest.*
(b) *On* Mallota cimbiciformis, *Fln.,* Stegana coleoptera, *Scop., and* Acletoxenus formosus, *Lw., at Cambridge.*
(c) *On* Coleoptera *at Cambridge.* Vol. xxxix, p. 227.

1904 *(a) *On* Asteia elegantula, *Zett., a Species of* Diptera *new to Britain.* Vol. xl, p. 4.
(b) *On* Loxocera fulviventris, *Mg., near Forres.* Vol. xl, p. 17.

1907 (a) *Habit of* Haematobia irritans.
(b) *On* Nephrocerus flavicornis, *Zett., at Cambridge.*
(c) *On* Xylomyia marginata, *Mg., at Cambridge.* Vol. xlii, pp. 13, 14.

1908 *Notes on certain Mycetophilidae, *including several species new to the British List.* Vol. xliv, pp. 129–133, 151–154.

1909 *On* Epicypta trinotata, *Staeg., a Correction (to the preceding paper).* Vol. xlv, p. 280.

1912 *On* Syntemna (?) alpicola, *Strobl (a new British species), in Morayshire.* Vol. xlviii, p. 67.

1913 (a) *Wasp attacking Peacock Butterfly.*
(b) *On* Opomyza lineatopunctata, *v.Ros., at Crowborough.* Vol. xlix, pp. 64, 65.

Cf. also "Transactions of Entom. Soc." 1896, pp. 233–252; 1913, pp. 334–381. *W. D. Lang,* "Handbook of British Mosquitoes," 1920, p. 109; *Map of distribution of Anopheles,* 1918, p. 8. *E. Meyrick,* Tineina taken by the late Dr Jenkinson. "Entomologist," vol. lviii, 1925, p. 259.

§ V. MISCELLANEOUS.

1883 *On the Music* to "The Birds." "Saturday Review," Dec. 8.

1915 *Obituary Notice of G. C. Macaulay.* "Cambridge Chronicle," July 16.

1919 *Obituary Notice of H. G. Aldis.* "New Cambridge," March 8.

1922 *Obituary Notice of A. B. Farn.* "Entom. Month. Mag." vol. lviii, pp. 20–22.

1923 *On Hicks of Bodmin.* "Sunday Times," Sept. 2.

APPENDIX II

THE 2nd number (March 21) of *U. L. C.*, a short periodical record of Library doings which, under the general editorship of C. E. Sayle, ran from 1920 to 1923 contained the following statement:

THE WAR COLLECTION

During the past five years an effort has been made to gather together the propaganda and other war literature which has been circulated throughout the different countries of the world, and thus to form a War Collection worthy of the Library.

The Collection may be roughly estimated to consist of about 10,000 items. In addition to the books and pamphlets received under the Copyright Act, and those acquired by purchase, a large number of pieces (including some of the most interesting in the Collection) have been obtained from contributors, numbering upwards of 650. These contributions are due entirely to the enthusiasm and energy of the Librarian, who has in most cases made a personal appeal to the donors. We are greatly indebted to all those who have interested themselves in our work, and helped to preserve these memorials of the great War.

The Library was particularly fortunate in enlisting the co-operation and assistance of Mr Stephen Gaselee, C.B.E., M.A., who was able to secure for us many valuable accessions. From Mr Benjamin Barrios, Señor F. Carbonell (Spain), Mr Charles S. Davison (America), Señor Dr R. Monteiro y Paullier (Uruguay), Señor G. D. Ricaurte (Colombia), Miss Phillpotts (Sweden), Major W. L. Murphy (Macedonia), we have received regular supplies of propaganda.

Immense quantities of foreign newspapers, which had been used for the compilation of the various sections of the "Review of the Foreign Press," were sent from the Foreign Office. These have been sorted into their various languages and countries of origin, arranged in chronological order, and given finding numbers, so that they may be readily accessible to the student.

Among the novelties which form part of the Collection may be mentioned two balloons received from Viscount Esher, used for the distribution of propaganda leaflets over the enemy lines; a large number of War Posters from T. Knox-Shaw, M.A., Lt. J. G. A. North, and others, some of which were obtained from hoardings in the occupied territory; postcards and letters from prisoners of war; regimental Christmas cards; a specimen of a cheap novel in Low German, in which is inserted a sheet of printed matter containing news of internal affairs in Germany—these were sent through the post to officers and men in prisoners' camps in this and other countries; Bolshevik paper money; local credit notes issued in France and Belgium, and many other items.

The Collection is divided into three main divisions:

(i) Events leading up to the outbreak of the War.
(ii) The Events of the War.
(iii) Matters arising out of the War.

These three divisions are represented by the Classes 537, 538, and 539, and for less important English War books, and volumes of classified pamphlets (English and Foreign), by the Class 9537. These classes stand in the open Library, and are accessible to readers. The larger portion of the Collection, being of an ephemeral nature, does not stand on the open shelves, but is placed in the Reserved Classes WRA—WRE. The three main divisions, as set out above, are subdivided, classified, and have a distinguishing number for each subject. By this arrangement the class-catalogue forms a subject-index to the whole Collection. A separate card-catalogue has been made, arranged under authors, and in the case of anonymous works, under the first word of the title, of all the War literature contained in the Library. This catalogue may be referred to by application in the Librarian's Room.

Posters are placed in WRP, and Newspapers in WRN.

The following table shows the plan of classification:

DIVISION I. 537

General history; Causes, origins; Diplomatic and other official documents; Political history.

DIVISION II. 538

Military operations (General).
,,   ,,   Western theatre.
,,   ,,   Eastern and Italian theatre.
,,   ,,   Asia and Africa.
Naval, aerial, and tank operations.
Auxiliary Services (Recruiting, Munitions, Red Cross, etc.).
Vandalism, atrocities, prisoners, etc.

DIVISION III. 539

International relations, neutral attitude and action.
Propaganda and pacifist literature.
Peace, overtures and negotiations.
Finance and economics of the War.
History and conditions in particular countries during the War.
Miscellaneous.

WRA—WRE (Reserved Classes)

DIVISION I: Parliamentary papers, Diplomatic correspondence and official documents; Political, historical, and philosophical literature.

DIVISION II: Military operations; Naval operations; Aerial operations; Auxiliary services; German occupation, deportation, vandalism; Prisoners, atrocities; Personal narratives, reminiscences; Regimental records, etc.; Illustrated albums, photographs, cartoons.

DIVISION III: Economics, finance, socialism; Official publications; Russian affairs, Bolshevism; Pacifist literature; Propaganda. (*a*) Allied, (*b*) German; Sermons, charities, religion, benevolent societies; Handbills, leaflets (General); Christmas cards, picture postcards; Social life, sports and amusements; Peace, League of Nations; Literature (Trench and Camp); Newspaper cuttings; Rolls of Honour; Reconstruction; Miscellaneous; Bibliography.

APPENDIX III

Composed by F. J.

Carolus Gulielmus King
Huius collegii
e sociis senioribus
In Cambria ortus
Obiit apud Londinenses
Die mensis Martii xxv
Anno salutis MDCCCLXXXVIII
Et in coemeterio
Iuxta Highgate sepultus est
De lapidum natura et artificio
Permulta egregie scripsit
Vixit annos LXIX
Simplex lepidus facundus
Sermone scriptis moribus
Domum quam vivus ingenio illustravit
Beneficio moriens ditavit.

M.S.

Henricus Richards Luard, S.T.P.
Huius collegii socius
Idemque in testamento benefactor,
Registrarius Academiae,
Ecclesiae S. Mariae Majoris diu vicarius,
Vixit annos LXV
Decessit anno M⁰DCCC⁰XCI⁰
Ipso die SS. Philippi et Iacobi.
Erat in re litteraria explorator
Curiosus acer indefessus,
Annalium custos ordinator editor insignis.
Specimen hospitalitatis amicitiae vera effigies
Sibi soli moriendo non displicuit.
Iuxta uxorem,
Sine qua vivere nec voluit nec potuit,
In coemeterio S. Aegidii requiescit:
Cuius animae propitietur Deus.

M.S.

MICHAEL FOSTER
Eques auratus
Societatis regiae socius insignis
Et diu secretarius
Londinensis academiae suffragiis
In Parliamento burgensis
Obiit anno post Christum MDCCCCVII°
Aetatis suae LXX°
Die mensis Ianuarii XXVIII°
Desideratissimus.
Erat huius collegii socius et aliquando
Praelector. Deinde in Academia Physio-
logiae Primus Professor novique studii
Novae disciplinae Inventor.
Qualis ipse fuerit quid effecerit
Testatur Academia testantur amici
Testantur vbique gentium
Scientiae tradentes lampada discipuli.

Composed by J. D. DUFF

FRANCISCUS IOANNES HENRICUS JENKINSON
Collegii socius et lector latinus
Inde in Academia per VI fere lustra
Bibliothecarius
Natus apud Forres Moraviae ad XIII kal. Sept. MDCCCLIII
Obiit Londinii ad XI kal. Oct. MDCCCCXXIII
Et in coemeterio de Trumpington quiescit.

Multarum erat disciplinarum peritus
Nullius fere non studiosus:
Raram sensuum mentisque aciem
Cum animi candore vultusque venustate
Ad ipsum vitae finem pertulit:
Naturam musicam libros
Sed magis homines homo amavit.

Beati mundo corde quoniam ipsi Deum videbunt

INDEX

For EU product safety concerns, contact us at Calle de José Abascal, 56–1°,
28003 Madrid, Spain or eugpsr@cambridge.org.

www.ingramcontent.com/pod-product-compliance
Ingram Content Group UK Ltd.
Pitfield, Milton Keynes, MK11 3LW, UK
UKHW010047140625
459647UK00012BB/1674